THE JOSHUA 24 EXPERIENCE

MIKE BAKER

THE JOSHUA 24 EXPERIENCE

iUniverse books may be ordered through booksellers or by contacting:

iUniverse
1663 Liberty Drive
Bloomington, IN 47403
www.iuniverse.com
1-800-Authors (1-800-288-4677)

ISBN: 978-1-5320-5133-3 (sc)
ISBN: 978-1-5320-5134-0 (e)

Library of Congress Control Number: 2018906467

Print information available on the last page.

iUniverse rev. date: 06/01/2018

INTRODUCTION

For the past ten years, the fearless followers of Eastview Christian Church have taken intentional growth steps together through movements we have called "all church studies." These structured times of pursuing our vision, supported with extensive study resources, have been successful in both growing our culture of small groups and taking us deeper in our faith. It is our conviction that "The Joshua 24 Experience" will do much the same. But from the first stages of prayer, study, preparation, and planning, the Spirit seemed to be calling us to something other than "just another all church study."

Of course, this study, like the others, will involve some reading, teaching, inspiration, and instruction from the Word. However, we wanted to do more than study the word – more than just walk away with more knowledge about our faith. What was that "more" we were looking for? In the end, the word that helped us define what we hoped to accomplish is the word "experience." Our desire is that everyone in our church family (and beyond) lives, practices, and participates in the themes of Joshua 24 over the next forty days. Therefore, this is not an "all church study" through Joshua 24, but "The Joshua 24 Experience" because we want you to experience the final chapter of Joshua in three ways.

EXPERIENCE IT PERSONALLY

First, and foremost this 40-day experience must be personal. We have no doubt that God wants to move in each individual, which means that you will need to commit to daily scriptures and readings as we examine the themes of Joshua 24. But this is not just another reading assignment. Since God has made each of us with unique design and purpose, we have limited each daily reading to about five minutes (even for slow readers like me) so that you can personalize your experience by writing in the spaces provided throughout. This means that by the time you have finished this book, much of the book will be about you and your personal Joshua 24 Experience. For this reason, we are asking each person to have his or her own copy of this book. If you are currently sharing this book with someone else (even your spouse), please make sure to get you own copy for a richer personal experience.

EXPERIENCE IT BY CUSTOMIZING YOUR OWN TENT

Second, you will want to experience Joshua 24 in community. This is where it gets fun; you get to choose those you want to experience it with. Using the desert-nomadic feel of Joshua, we have labeled these customized groups as your "tent" - your closest circle of family or friends, an intimate place for doing life together. Of course, we still believe that small groups (even the most imperfect ones) are the best way to experience faith, and so you may opt to go through Joshua 24 with your current small group, by forming a new group, or joining another group. As usual, we will assist you in this endeavor.

However, for the first time, we are offering a wide variety of options for those who might desire a tent that is different from a small group. Here are some possibilities that may appeal to you: Many will choose the tent of their home, experiencing Joshua 24 with mom, dad and siblings, or roommates. Others may choose a group of fellow students before school or an experience with associates at your place of employment. Perhaps you will choose to join us in a larger group setting at our building throughout the week, or you might prefer starting a group in your neighborhood. The point is that you choose a tent and participate weekly during the 40-day experience. In the back of this book we have provided tools specifically written for your group or family tent experience. Again, the goal is participating together. Please don't miss out by choosing a tent of one. Other seekers and followers of God will enhance this experience.

EXPERIENCE IT WITH THE CHURCH

Finally, you will want to participate each Sunday of the forty days for unique experiences as we gather for worship as a body. During each week our worship services will be designed to encourage the expression of your faith in a variety of ways. This will include, among other things: confession, publicly choosing God, baptism, a multi-generations worship experience, and a service of putting away the things that get in God's way. The ultimate Sunday experience will take place on the fourth Sunday of our journey with an all-church recommitment that will include the dedication of a stone monument similar to the one we find in Joshua 24.

We invite you to join us for the forty days of The Joshua 24 Experience. Our prayer is that when this experience is over, we will not have just observed God from a distance, but that we will have walked with him, experienced his love through Christ, and have new resolve to experience him daily. With that goal in mind, and many prayers for God to move in us, let the experience begin.

DAY 1 - REMEMBER

Joshua 24:2&3

"And Joshua said to all the people, 'Thus says the Lord, the God of Israel, 'Long ago, your fathers lived beyond the Euphrates, Terah, the father of Abraham and of Nahor, and they served other gods. Then I took your father Abraham from beyond the River and led him throughout the land of Canaan, and made his offspring many.'"

I have a tendency to forget things. Call it A.D.D., short attention span, a beautiful mind, or...what was I talking about? Oh yeah. Forgetfulness. There is a pattern in my life of forgetting even the simplest of things. Maybe you have, like me, walked into a room to get something only to find yourself frozen in place wondering what you came to get. I often ask my wife to repeat the name of a person she just introduced me to... 15 seconds ago... for the tenth time. For those who have seen me preach, you know I can forget where I am in a sermon from just about any distraction in the worship center.

To overcome this forgetfulness of mine, I intentionally use a variety of reminders to help me remember the important things in my life. I always set important items on top of my car keys making it impossible (almost impossible) to drive off without remembering to take them with me. I set alarm reminders on my phone to make sure I remember out-of-office appointments. Sometimes, I talk to myself repeating my objective for entering a room until it is accomplished: "get the tickets, get the tickets, get the tickets." I often write my prayers so that I'll remember to focus on conversation with God. I am not alone in these remembering techniques. My wife, Sara, uses post-it notes when we are getting ready to travel. On the bathroom mirror, the refrigerator, and throughout the house, little pink and yellow pieces of paper help her remember: "get medicine, go to bank, pick up dry cleaning, or buy new shoes." (Okay, I threw that last one in for fun, she doesn't need a reminder for shoes!)

The point is that Sara and I are not alone. We all have a tendency to forget things we need to remember. And if this is true in our day-to-day living, then it is very likely true in the day-to-day spirituality. If we are honest, most of us Christ followers would have to admit that we suffer from a sort of spiritual amnesia, a tendency to forget important things related to God and our faith journey. I believe this is Joshua's concern as he begins his farewell address and it will be our focus as we begin our Joshua 24 experience. "To be continued" implies that there is more to the story, the people and the kingdom of God are moving forward. However, to do so, God's children must remember all the ways in which God has guided them. This is why Joshua begins with a 450-year historical review of God's work in their lives and while he doesn't actually use the word, there are two distinct things he wants them to remember.

Remember where you came from.

Joshua doesn't begin with the recent history of the Israelites; he takes them back further to a "long ago" time when there were no "people of God." Remember that Abraham's dad and family were citizens of a pagan world beyond the great Euphrates River in modern day Iraq. This ancient place, called Ur, has undergone extensive archeological research that has revealed among other things: royal palaces, a ziggurat (think pyramid with a flat top), a royal tomb, signs of wealth and economy, and evidence of human sacrifice. This is Abraham's hometown. The great father of many nations was first a regular guy who was likely caught up in the worldly and sinful ways of his culture. Joshua indicates he and his family were idol worshippers noting, "they served other gods." How did Abraham get out of there? God chose him and took him out. You may want to take a few minutes and read Joshua 24:1-13 to see all the places the people of God were before God delivered them.

Joshua recites the history of the people of God reminding them of where Isaac had been, the journey of Esau and Jacob, and the calling of Moses and Aaron. Fast forward to the people who now lived in the land of promise and he reminds them of their recent history, where they had literally come from. They had been slaves in Egypt for 400 years under Pharaoh's rule. They had been wanderers in the desert of rebellion for 40 years. They had been strangers in a land surrounded with kings who wanted to destroy them. But, by the grace of God, they were living in the inheritance he had promised.

In order for the current people of God to move forward, we too must remember where we came from. I'm not talking about our hometowns per se, although that may be part of it. What I want us to reflect on as we begin this "to be continued" study together is where we came from spiritually. What were we before Jesus? I realize that some, like me, were raised in the church and can't really recall a time before Jesus. But, we certainly weren't perfect! What were you before you got serious about making a commitment about Jesus? What sin really held you down as a kid, in high school, in college, or last week? What pain have you endured and relationships have you had? What experiences shaped your early life and feelings about God? What family did you grow up in? This is your story. To the best of your recollection, who were you, where were you, and what were you without Jesus?

Remember what God has done to get you where you are.

Joshua understood the greatness of God's salvation to be contingent on what God has done to get us from where we were to where we are. He reminds the people that Abraham was a father because God "made his offspring many (24:3)," He reminds them that during the slavery, "I [God] plagued Egypt, and afterward I brought you out (24:5)." He tells them to remember how their "eyes saw what I [God] did in Egypt (24:7)." Joshua recalls how the Amorites "fought with you, and I gave them into your hand (24:8)." Joshua says on behalf of God: "I delivered you (24:10)." "I sent the hornet before you (24:12)," and "I gave you a land (24:13)." And one other reminder, "It was not by your sword or by your bow." In other words, the Old Testament people of God are now in the land of promise because of all God has done and not by anything they have done.

This is, of course, the gospel message. Everything we are in Christ is because of the work he did on the cross to take away our sin and overcome our death. "For the wages of sin is death, but the gift of God is eternal life through Jesus Christ our Lord." (Romans 6:23). And now we are destined to live as children of God who are a part of his kingdom, his church, his family – saints who will spend eternity in his presence. In light of all his provision and how he has delivered us, our challenge as we begin this experience is to remember. Remember where you have come from and where you currently are and take a few minutes to reflect on God's work in your life to this point. As you do, write these parts of your story on the page provided below. Also, please refer to the appropriate study guide in the back of this book for additional spiritual exercises during this week of remembering.

Day 1 - Remember

DAY 2 - GOD REMEMBERS

Exodus 2:24

"And God heard their groaning, and God remembered
his covenant with Abraham, Isaac, and Jacob. God
saw the people of Israel-and God knew."

It had been about 500 years since God made an agreement
with Abraham. He was an old and childless man when God
makes the promise in Genesis 12:2: "I will make of you a great
nation." Along with this promise of family, God covenanted with
Abraham to prosper him, to give him the land he would walk
through, and to overcome all his enemies. He made the same
covenant with Abraham's son Isaac and grandson Jacob. But,
from a worldly perspective, God had only kept the part of the
agreement about making Abraham a great nation. Based on the
number of fighting men that eventually leave Egypt (600,000 –
Exodus 12:37), we estimate that this family that had come to
Egypt as 12 sons of Jacob and 70 people total had now grown into
a nation of 2-3 million people!

On the other hand, these people of God had been oppressed
by the Egyptians and their Pharaohs (who had not known Joseph
and were afraid of Israel's increasing population) for 400 years.
The Egyptians made their existence a living hell of harsh bondage,

described with words like "ruthless," "bitter," and "hard service" (see Exodus 1:13&14). Day after day, year after year, and generation after generation, these descendants of Abraham clung to the other part of the promise that God would deliver them and lead them to the land their forefathers had walked nearly half a millennia before. Can you imagine their prayers? They cried out. They pleaded. They fasted. They prayed. They sought God, and they prayed some more. Could it be that God had forgotten his people and his promise?

This is the human perspective. A perspective and questions that are as common now with us as they were 3,500 years ago. God has forgotten me. God has forgotten his promises. God must not care. God must not see. How can a loving God… (Write your God-sized expectations or disappointments here)? Maybe God should have tied a string on his finger or set a cosmic timer so that he wouldn't have forgotten. Five hundred years is a long time and you know God isn't getting any younger. So we think. However, God didn't "remember" his covenant because it slipped his mind and the people had to remind him. He remembered it in the sense that he acted in his people's interest with timing that finally lined up with theirs.

It's easy to think that God has forgotten. Why? Because so much of our lives and our world seems godless. From bad hair days to baby starving; from girls kidnapped for sex slavery to murder in our cities; from math tests to cancer tests, and from broken bones to broken hearts. Our lives can be as bitter, ruthless, and hard as the slavery in Egypt. And, we cry out for God to fix it, change it, do something. Three verbs from our reading give me hope today. No matter what my life or this world looks like, God doesn't forget and he hasn't forgotten.

God hears. How many prayers had the children of Israel prayed in 400 years of slavery? How many tent-group prayer requests to end slavery and oppression? How many times had they pleaded for relief from the painful sting of the taskmaster's whip? How many prayers for God to judge and punish the enemy

Egyptians? Hello? God aren't you listening? The temptation with prayer is to think that if God doesn't answer in our time and our way, he isn't listening. But, he hears every prayer. He hears the preschooler kneeling bedside and talking to him about everything from bugs to pillows. He hears the prisoner ask for forgiveness. He hears the abused cry for help. He hears the requests for blessing food and supplying food. It is impossible to address God and not get his attention. Maybe the hearing problem is the other way around. Maybe we get so busy asking for stuff, we don't hear God saying, "I'm here," "Soon," "Hang on," "It will all be better," and "I love you." If you're crying out to God right now because of some pain or affliction, might I suggest you take some time to listen to him today? It may be helpful to go back to the blank pages you wrote on yesterday and list some things you would like God to change. Now, listen. Write down what you imagine him saying.

God sees. He sees everything. He sees the deterioration of a terminal illness, but he also sees the beauty of a dad giving his girl away at her wedding. He sees the mean people you do, but he also witnesses millions (billions)? of kind acts by his people. He sees racism but he also sees people of different color embracing and loving one another. He sees death & murder-attends every funeral, but he also orchestrates and witnesses every baby born into the world full of life, hope, and potential. He sees the smog, but he sees the colorful kaleidoscope of birds, skies, fish, and flowers all over the world. He sees drugs abused, but he also sees doctors use drugs to save lives. He sees it all. Me. You. Everyone.

God knows. Since God sees and hears everything, he knows everything. One of the most comforting verses in the Bible is Matthew 6:8 that says God "knows what you need before you ask." "Hey God, you know about that test I failed?" Yep. "Hey God, you remember when I said I would start going to church?" Yep. "Lord, right now I feel like…" I know. "God my dad is…" I know. "God, I wanted to let you know I struggle with this sin." Yes, I know. There is nothing I can say to God about my world, my life, my feelings, my pain, my disappointment, or my fears that he doesn't know.

Why am I so sure he still hears, sees, and knows? Because of his greatest act of love. He loved us so much, he sent his son Jesus – personally experiencing, hearing, seeing, and knowing the human condition. It may seem like he has forgotten sometimes, but he paid too high of a price to forget. He came once to save us and soon, when the time is right, he will "remember" his covenant to save us from the slavery of the sin and death of this world and will come again to take us out of here.

DAY 3 - REMEMBER THE SABBATH

Exodus 20:8-11

"Remember the Sabbath day, to keep it holy. Six days you shall labor, and do all your work, but the seventh day is a Sabbath to the Lord your God. On it you shall not do any work, you or your son, or your daughter, your male servant, or your female servant, or your livestock, or the sojourner within your gates. For in six days the Lord made the heaven and the earth, the sea and all that is in them, and rested on the seventh day. Therefore the Lord blessed the Sabbath day and made it holy."

A tight publishing schedule and deadline found me writing the beginning to this chapter on my day off. Then it hit me. I'm writing about remembering the Sabbath and here I am ignoring the rest day that God wants for me. So I stopped writing right here. [The next day] Well, I am back to writing and I have to say my mind is fresher and my soul is more at peace because of the rest day I just practiced. Of course, God isn't surprised. Rest is so important to him that he created a sacred day each week just for relaxing. Though we Christ-followers may not be required to observe the specific ritual of Saturday, I believe God still wants us to remember the principle of rest behind it.

The word Sabbath doesn't mean Saturday, although even in

modern Israeli culture their word for Saturday is "shabat" – a Hebrew word that originally meant to "pause" or "rest." In other words, the seventh day of the week (the day we call Saturday) was designed for the people of God as a day to push the pause button on life. And, although this day has significance in the spiritual sense, I believe there is also a practical side to this weekly day off. However, before we get to that, let's examine quickly why most Christians no longer observe a Sabbath day of rest on a specific day.

In the Old Testament, there are three kinds of laws outlined in the law handed down from Moses (Genesis through Exodus, or what Jews call "the Torah"). There are _civic laws_ that help keep a society safe and functioning. For example, how many sheep do you have to pay back if you are caught stealing one? Much of these laws are what we might call "case law" based on actual cases Moses had to judge. Along with these, there are _ceremonial laws_ that involve ritual designed to point a person to God. The most obvious of these would be the sacrificial system that required specific animals to be sacrificed. Finally, there are _moral laws._ These laws reflect the eternal person of God and are right for all people in all places for all time. An example would be the Ten Commandments.

So, how do we know which laws are which and where does the Sabbath fall in this discussion? The best way for us to understand our Christian living is to look at the early church and see what those first believers did with the Old Testament laws. Remember, Jesus' church was birthed out of the Jewish faith, so nearly all of the early church and her leaders were thoroughly Jewish and would not have broken a law they thought important or crucial to faith. Concerning the civic laws, Paul is very clear that we should be subject (as much as it doesn't conflict with our faith in Jesus) to the governing authorities (Romans 13:1). So the civic laws of the nation we live in are the ones we are subject to (yeah, this includes speed limits).

That brings us to the Sabbath day (technically from sundown Friday to sundown Saturday) and what we Christians are supposed to do with it. On one hand, the early church seems to have gradually moved away from adherence to the ritual of Saturday as a holy day, preferring Sunday instead. This first day of the week was referred to as "the Lord's day" throughout the New Testament, marking both the day Jesus rose from the dead and the birth of the church on the Day of Pentecost. On the other hand, the early church (not to mention our Lord Jesus) seems to have practiced a regular "shabat" of rest and worship in the Christ-following lives. A safe conclusion would be that a day of rest is still a practical moral law from God for us and at the same time, not ceremonially required to be practiced on a Saturday.

There are two thoughts to pray about today as you think through this "remember the Sabbath" instruction. The first is your need for the physical rest of a weekly Sabbath. God did not design the human body to work every day of the week. As I've said to some high capacity members of my staff, "You may be exceptional, but you're not the exception." We all need rest. You need rest. I need rest (yes, I am convicted even as I write). However, from my pastoral vantage point, most of us are tired. Parents are tired. Students are tired. Volunteers are tired. Church staff is tired. We are a sleep-deprived people. For your physical well-being, would you join me and prayerfully consider making some schedule changes so that we can live fully as God intended and find rest in him?

The second thought for consideration is your spiritual need for a weekly Sabbath. God's idea of rest is designed for your soul as much as for your body. We know that God wasn't physically tired when he rested. He wasn't at the end of his strength. He didn't exclaim to the angels T.M.I.F (Thank me it's Friday). God's rest was spiritual. He paused to take it all in. He took a breath to reflect. He stopped to enjoy the new creation. And this is why we need to rest as well. Since we are made in the image of God, with his very breath in us; our souls also need to reflect. We need to slow down long enough to enjoy family, food, nature, slow conversation, and most importantly turn our thoughts toward God.

So, how are you doing with this spiritual discipline? Take a few minutes to go back to the journal pages and note the day you normally reserve for "rest." What do you do on that day? Could you use some rest? Be honest as you assess where you are. Talk to God about changes you need to make to "remember the Sabbath day to keep it holy."

DAY 4 - REMEMBER FREEDOM
Deuteronomy 15:15

"You shall remember that you were a slave in the land of Egypt, and the Lord your God redeemed you; therefore I command you this today."

Today's verse comes in the middle of a very long speech from the "great law giver" Moses on how to govern the people of God in regards to the treatment of debtors, servants, and the poor. And, while these laws establish very practical civil (see explanation from yesterday's reading) boundaries, there is a very valuable, moral, and eternal truth revealed as well. A truth that we follow because we remember.

The law of the seventh year was commanded by God to forgive all debts and free all slaves every seven years among the people of God: "At the end of every seven years you shall grant a release" (Deuteronomy 15:1). The word translated "release" in our English versions is a Hebrew word (shem it ta') that literally means "to drop." The requirement for the people of Israel was that if you owned a slave, you "dropped" the rights to them and if someone owed you money, you "dropped" their debt. Along with this, the command included a rule of generosity toward the poor in the sixth year as one anticipated less income for the seventh year.

This practical "dropping" by the people of God every seven

years illustrated God's eternal desire for us to be free. He is, always has been, and always will be for our freedom, and he goes to great lengths to ensure we ultimately have it. You may question, "Why then, didn't he just outlaw slavery?" Was God okay with slaves? The short answer is "no." Everything we know about God's personality is that he shows no favoritism toward one human over another. All are created in his image. However, his created human race is sinful and that sin leads to oppression, slavery, and poverty. Therefore, these civil laws were not an endorsement of slavery, but a means to end slavery and give freedom on a regular basis.

The Israelites were slaves in Egypt. How quickly the people of God (then and now) are prone to forget where they come from. There was a time in Hebrew history when these Promised Land inhabitants were children who watched as their parents collapsed under the weight of bondage. They heard their parents curse the Egyptian masters, beg for mercy, and pray to God for deliverance. Now that this second generation out of Egypt had settled in a good land and found themselves prospering by God's provision, they were becoming the oppressors they once despised. God says, "**Remember** that you were a slave…"

We were slaves to sin. It's a good reminder to remember that we too were slaves. You may not think you were ever a slave, but Jesus said we were because of our sin. "Truly, truly, I say to you, everyone who practices sin is a *slave to sin*" (John 8:34). Every one of our stories before Jesus is a story of slavery because all of us were sinners. Some of us were enslaved by lust, seeking love and pleasure through constant sexual activity – compelled to return repeatedly to something that made us feel empty and alone. Some of us were enslaved by money, greed, or possessions, and yet the more we accumulated the more we wanted, never satisfied – slaves to "more." Still others came from bondage to drugs, food, alcohol, or some other addictive substance. In our collective pasts, we've done time in the jail cell of selfishness, been handcuffed by our lying, incarcerated by envy, and weighed down with hate. Paul clarifies this in Titus 3:3 where he writes, "For we ourselves were once foolish, disobedient, led astray, _slaves to various passions and pleasures_, passing our days in malice and envy, hated by others and hating one another."

One casualty of long term Christianity is that Christ followers forget how bad our lives were before Jesus and begin to look down on others. We begin to think that we are better than other sinners and that our enslavement was never as bad. And, in a weird distortion of the grace we have been given, we enslave others by our haughty judgement. There are some people in the world who will not come into Christian circles for fear that they will be required to pay for their sins that are overwhelming. All the while, we should be offering the freedom of redemption that we received.

The Israelites were redeemed. God tells these Old Testament people of God to remember that he had redeemed them. The word redeemed means "to set free" and the implication is that a price or ransom has to be paid for that freedom. God redeemed his people from Egypt by the blood of the Passover lamb on the night he destroyed all the firstborn in Egypt. The price for their freedom was a firstborn son. Do you see where this is going?

Now we are free. You and I have been redeemed in the same way. When we were slaves to sin and condemned to die in our slavery, God gave his son (the Lamb of God) to pay for a debt we could never get out from under. Romans 6:22 says, "But now that you have been _set free from sin_ and have become slaves of God, the fruit you get leads to sanctification and its end, eternal life." Thankfully, we have been set free from our sin so that we can freely submit to serving God. This is freedom and this is something we should remember.

DAY 5 - FORGET IT

Isaiah 43:25

"I, I am he who blots out your transgressions for my own sake, and **I will not remember** *your sins."*

One of the greatest tools of my ministry, aside from the Bible, is undoubtedly the white board that hangs on the wall in my office. A day does not go by without me scribbling the jumble of thoughts, words, impressions, inspirations, and tasks that seem to swirl constantly through my mind. This allows me (with a variety of colored markers) to creatively visualize sermon ideas, word structures, prayer emphases, vision expressions, and upcoming projects. However, the best part is not that I can write on the board, but that I can erase things from it. With the wipe of a soft cloth, I can eliminate bad ideas, completed projects, and answered prayers, leaving a clean space for my next "great" idea. On occasion I will erase everything leaving a white surface with no markings on it all. Once the former ideas are erased, they're gone. No evidence they ever existed. Can't retrieve them. No reversing it. Things that will not be remembered.

If you glance at this white board illustration with just a slight spiritual squint, you will see our verse for today. This is how it is with our sin. Pretend with me a minute. Think of your life, all of it,

18

from birth to death, as a giant white board where every sin you ever committed or will commit is recorded. Visible evidence of every failed promise, every sinful act, every broken rule, every hurtful word, and every selfish motive written in black ink. Now think of today's verse translated in this context. "I, I am he who wipes your whiteboard clean. Because I want to, I choose not to remember all the bad stuff you've done." This is simple, but profound. God, the one who remembers his covenant, chooses to forget our sin! Let's try to understand this verse and this forgetting.

Our sin is against God. Two words of note here describe exactly what God is erasing from our lives. The words "transgressions" and "sins" in our verse are two of many words that describe offense against God in the Bible – each with slightly nuanced meaning. The general word for "sin" (as here) is a word that means to "miss the mark" or "go the wrong way." In other words, sin is to miss God's mark of righteousness or to go our own way ignoring God's way. Of course, this is what we often do with our relationships, our money, our careers, and our time. We go our way and miss God's way. We all have missed God's mark. Or, as the prophet says, "we like sheep have gone astray" (Isaiah 53:6). The other word in this verse is a little more intense. "Transgression" denotes a willful rebellion against God. A choice to defect from him and in essence declare ourselves to be his equal. To grasp the wonder of this verse, we must understand that we have offended God with our rebellion and wandering.

He blots out our sin for his sake. This whole sin/forgiveness thing is not about us, it's about God. All throughout the 43rd chapter of Isaiah, God emphasizes that he stands uniquely above everything by repetition of the pronoun "I". Thirty times in 28 verses, with courtroom language, God makes a case for his greatness. And it's compelling: "I have called you" (v. 1), "I will be with you (v. 2), "I am the Lord" (vs. 3, 11, 15), "I created" and "I formed" (v. 7), "I have chosen" (v. 10), "I work" (v.13), "I am doing a new thing" (v. 19), and "I will make a way" (v. 19). It is against Him that we have sinned. And, (don't miss this) he shouldn't, doesn't have to, and doesn't need to forgive our sin. But, this "great one" described by each of the "I" phrases mentioned above forgets our sins "for his own sake". Because he created us, formed us, and chose us, he loves us. He forgets it! And, this love drives him to act in grace without compromising justice. Moreover, this great work of salvation in our lives further glorifies his name because ultimately, he is the only one whose greatness enables him to do something unbelievable with our sin. The taking away of our sin does not point to how great we are because we are sinless, it points to a God who is even greater than all our sin.

He blots out our sin by his work. Finally, in our verse for the day, we find a word that helps explain how God gets rid of our sin. The expression "blots out" is a Hebrew term (ma kha) that was used in ancient times in connection with accounting books. Yes, in ancient times they kept records of debt on a variety of surfaces and some of these surfaces were capable of being blotted out for reuse. That's what makes this word so intriguing. At the root of it, "blots out" really means to "rub or rub over". In other words to erase. So, when the people heard the prophet Isaiah say that God would "blot out" their transgressions they understood it to be an erasing of their debt of sin recorded in God's eternal record books.

In the New Testament we find the instrument God uses for this blotting out work. Paul writes in Colossians 2:13b and following "… God made us alive together with him, having forgiven us all our trespasses, by canceling the record of debt that stood against us with it's legal demands. This he set aside, nailing it to the cross." In other words, God used the sacrifice of his son on the cross to erase all our sin, all our debt and all that we owe him because of our rebellion. In one historic swipe God took my sin, your sin, and the sin of the world away, which is why he will not remember our sins – he has taken them away – they no longer exist.

Many of us struggle to move on from our collective pasts, but we need to. I realize that the problem is that we still suffer some of the consequences of our former sins and that makes them hard to forget. But, when we struggle with our past, we should remember that God struggled for us by the death of his son on the cross to erase our sin and get rid of it forever. Today, let's do what God has done with our sin. Forget it.

DAY 6 - IN REMEMBRANCE

Luke 22:19&20

---

*"And he took the bread, and when he had given thanks, he broke it and gave it to them, saying, 'This is my body, which is given for you. Do this **in remembrance** of me.' And likewise the cup after they had eaten, saying, 'This cup that is poured out for you is the new covenant in my blood.'"*

From my vantage point, third row back on the right side of the church sanctuary, I had to lean up or tilt my head into the aisle to see the words. These special words were carved in big block letters on a huge wooden table that in my memory seemed as big as a small car. On Sundays, this table was covered with a white cloth and gold colored trays stacked neatly. They were bookended with oversized fancy chairs that only elders could sit in. Obviously, as a grade schooler, I didn't fully understand the sacredness of the communion table, but the words were emblazoned on my mind: "**In remembrance** of me."

From the disciples' vantage point, reclining as usual for the festival meal, all but a few had to lean in and cup their ears to hear the words. These special words came from the lips of the man they had been following for three years and this Passover meal seemed different from any they had ever celebrated. On the table, the cups of wine, the unleavened bread of blessing, the bitter herbs, and the sacrificial lamb were prepared as usual for the annual celebration of Israel's deliverance from the bondage of Egypt. Obviously, these men did not fully understand how sacred this moment and this meal would become, but they would never forget the words that their Lord spoke that night while breaking bread and drinking wine: "Do this **in remembrance** of me."

From Gaius' vantage point, seated as usual on the steps in the courtyard of his Corinthian home, he could clearly see the group of 20-30 believers who had just finished their weekly fellowship meal commonly called "the love feast" (see I Corinthians 1:14). It was a mixed group of men and women, young and old, singles and families, rich and poor, who gathered in one of many Corinthian house churches on this Sunday. The meal followed its typical pattern of eating, talking, laughing, sharing, and celebrating, and was now to be concluded in characteristic fashion with the special celebration called "the Lord's supper." But, this Sunday afternoon was different. Paul's young assistant Timothy was in town (see I Corinthians 16:10) to read a new epistle to the congregation who admittedly didn't fully understand what this sacred meal was all about. As his words surrounding the climax of the celebration echoed through the courtyard, the true meaning of this weekly church ritual was affirmed: "Do this **in remembrance** of me" (I Corinthians 11:24).

From the vantage point of many Christians in American churches today (including mine), the gold colored trays being passed down the aisles by the ushers hold small square pieces of bread and disposable plastic cups with a splash of grape juice. This weekly component of worship that is now a 2,000-year-old sacrament, is usually introduced by one of the pastors from the platform who shares a Scripture reminding us of the death, burial, and resurrection of Jesus. In addition, while many who partake of the symbols of Jesus' body and blood may not fully understand the eternal reality these emblems represent; the words still ring true: "Do this **in remembrance** of me."

With these four views of this ancient tradition of body and blood, I have tried to illustrate how the remembrance of the Lord's sacrifice has been celebrated throughout twenty centuries of church history. It is remarkably translated into every time and culture. Personally, I have partaken of the body and blood thousands of times. I have been privileged to share these emblems with brothers and sisters in India, Mexico, Dominican Republic, Morocco, Canada, New Zealand, Grenada, Haiti, Greece, Turkey, and Israel. And, in each case, the methods have varied widely but the remembering is the same.

The body of Christ has been represented in matzo crackers, tortilla shells, whole loaves, flat bread, and pita. The blood of Christ has been represented through red Kool-Aid, cranberry juice, wine and grape juice. I have taken it with a background of music in a plain-walled room in secret and among the trees of the Garden Tomb in Jerusalem. I have dipped the bread, broken the bread, and had the bread placed in my mouth. I have drunk from one shared cup, small glass cups and disposable cups. But whatever the elements used, one thing remains constant. It is about those words Jesus spoke at the first of all such meals: "Do this **in remembrance** of me."

In this week of remembering, it is more than appropriate to recall the sacrifice of Jesus through the picture of this ancient meal. In the same way he broke the bread, his body was broken through the abusive beatings and eventual crucifixion on the cross. And, in the same way, he poured the wine into the cup, his blood dripped "from his head, his hands, and his feet" as the old hymn proclaims. Jesus died for my sins on the cross. He took a beating for our arrogance. He bled for our murderous and hateful thoughts and words. He was broken for our lies and lust. He shed his last ounce of his precious life for our lives that were not worth much.

He breathed his last with us on his mind. And he simply calls us to regular remembrance of the price he paid. That is what I'm praying you will do today.

Take some time to reflect on your sin and remember the price he paid so that you could be sinless by faith in him. It may be helpful for you to read one of the crucifixion passages from the gospels. Just read an account of the cross and quietly reflect on its reality. Perhaps you will want to celebrate communion in your quiet time, or join with those in your tent for an experience that is "in remembrance."

DAY 7 - REMEMBER TO PRAY FOR OTHERS

Philemon 1:4

"I thank my God always when I remember you in my prayers."

Ephesians 1:16

"I do not cease to give thanks for you, remembering you in my prayers…"

"It is possible to move men, through God, by prayer alone." This quote, attributed to the famed China missionary Hudson Taylor, is one of two that I keep prominently on my desk. It is there to remind me that the most important (and likely the most powerful) thing I can do for another person is to pray for them. Amazingly, this tool that connects the Christ follower directly to the throne and heart of our Heavenly Father on behalf of another is often forgotten. So in this final experience in our week of remembering comes this reminder from the apostle Paul to remember to pray for others.

Truth is, prayer is not that hard. It's pretty natural to cry out to God. We say prayers before meals. We pray with our kids before they go to sleep. We pray for our kids when we can't sleep. We pray at church. We keep prayer lists. We pray when tragedy hits. We pray when we need something. We pray for all kinds of miraculous outcomes - from passing a test we didn't study for to healing from cancer. We pray in small groups. Athletes pray after games. Heck, even the United States Congress prays. But, in all of this, we sometimes don't remember to pray for the specific people in our lives.

The verses we read above should convict us to pray for others. In them, Paul is sincerely remembering people in prayer, but he is also setting us a spiritual example to follow. So, whom should we remember to pray for? Glad you asked, because the rest of this day's experience will reveal five scriptures of "ones" that we should all remember to pray for. As you read each of these, list the people in your life who fit each description.

Remember to pray for your pastors.

It may seem a bit self-serving for a pastor to ask for prayer, but it's biblical and we pastors need it. Throughout the years, it has been the prayers of thousands that have helped me preach, kept me from stumbling or quitting, and helped me grow in my faith. I can't wait to get to glory and see the millions of prayers God answered in my life. By the way, praying for your pastors makes you and your church better. When people tell me they don't get much out of their preacher's sermons, I ask them if they are praying for his sermons. Think of it, you can make your preacher better by praying for him and that, in the long run, is better for everyone. A prayer you can pray for this preacher is one Paul requested in Ephesians 6:18-20: "…[pray] also for me, that words may be given to me in opening my mouth boldly to proclaim the mystery of the gospel…that I may declare it boldly as I ought to speak."

My pastor(s):

Remember to pray for one another.

Broadly, all believers should be praying for all of the other two-billion-plus believers worldwide. However, each of us has relationships with specific Christ followers in our lives whom we should remember often in prayer. Start with your family. Pray for your spouse. Teens, pray for your parents. Parents, pray for your children and grandchildren. Remember each family member every day in prayer. Add to your family, close friends, co-workers, teammates and classmates. Remember them in prayer when they call, text, or as soon as you leave their presence. It doesn't have to be a long prayer. Just pray for them. Finally add brothers and sisters in your small group, those you serve with, and the missionaries your church supports. Do this regularly. This commitment for all believers to pray for one another is modeled in II Thessalonians where Paul says, "We always pray for you."

My "one anothers:"

Remember to pray for leaders in the community and country.

Next on the list of those to remember in prayer may surprise you, especially in the current political climate. It is easier to criticize, give opinions, and argue with government policy than it is to pray for those in charge, but that's what the Bible says we should do. In I Timothy 2:1-4 we are encouraged to pray "…for kings and all who are in high positions, that we may lead a peaceful and quiet life, godly and dignified in every way." Add local, state, national government officials to your prayer list. Think about this. If you don't think a government official is leading in a godly way and you know God can change anybody in any way, why aren't you talking to God about that official? This list also may include powerful business men and women.

My government leaders:

Remember to pray for the sick.

I would dare say that most prayer requests are health related so sick people asking for physical healing doesn't seem to be a problem. But, there is another kind of sickness. The healing James is talking about in his letter is both physical and spiritual. "Therefore, confess your sins to one another and pray for one another, that you may be healed." James 5:16. I know it is easier to tell someone that you've been having headaches than telling them you're struggling with pornography. But, we should get over this. Sick is sick. And healing comes when the people of God pray for those who are sick. I hope that you are close enough to some "other ones" you know who are sick in both ways. Pray for them to be healed of any physical ailment and the sins they have confessed to you.

My sick friends:

Remember to pray for those who are against you.

Finally, Jesus gives us an epic spiritual challenge. "Love your enemies and pray for those who persecute you" (Matthew 5:44). Wait. What? Are you serious? I can only assume Jesus meant it when he said these words, but why? I think it's this simple: hating our enemy is easy when we look at them through the lens of human experience, but when we take them into the presence of God, our perspective becomes eternal. And we change. And who knows, but that God will change them.

My enemies:

Now, you have a list of people to remember in prayer. Take some time to pray for them today and remember them tomorrow. And, while you're at it, pray for me. I prayed for you as I finished this chapter.

DAY 8 - CHOOSE

Joshua 24:15

---

*"And if it is evil in your eyes to serve the Lord, choose this day
whom you will serve, whether the gods your fathers served in the
region beyond the river, or the gods of the Amorites in whose land
you dwell. But as for me and my house, we will serve the Lord."*

Life is filled with choices. Every day, over and over, year after year,
each of us has a seemingly unlimited number of choices to make.

Some choices can seem quite frivolous and unimportant.
You have experienced this if you've dined in a restaurant and try
to simply order steak and a salad. Let the choices begin. What
seems simple now becomes a series of rapid-fire choices offered
by the server. Filet? New York Strip? Ribeye? How would you like
that prepared? Medium? Medium well? Rare? And, for your side?
Vegetables? Rice pilaf (personally, I don't trust the word "pilaf."
Is that French for "pile of" – but I digress – back to the choices.)
Fries? Regular or shoestring? Baked potato? Sour Cream? Butter?
Bacon? Salad? Caesar? Chopped? Garden? Dressing? French? And
to drink? By my calculations, we often make as many as 20 choices
just to get dinner!

Of course, there are other more important decisions we get to make over the course of our lives. What do you want to be when you grow up? Where would you like to go to college? What will you major in? Whom will you marry? Will you have children? How many? Where will you live? Should you take this job? Should you switch jobs? What kind of car will you drive? What kind of house can you live in? What are the rules for your kids? Drive the speed limit or not? What is your hobby? What do you do for entertainment? Are you a Cubs fan or Cardinals fan? (Reds thank you!) What form of exercise do you prefer? If you don't want to exercise, that's a choice too. You get to choose your doctor, how you spend your money, where you do your shopping, and whether or not you will homeschool your kids. All of the above doesn't begin to mention the number of daily decisions each of us make at work, school, and social settings.

I'm stressed just writing about all the decisions I have to make and maybe you are also, as you consider all there is to choose in life. Still we haven't even mentioned the most important lifetime choice any of us will ever make. In fact, it's a decision we have to make. There are no passes. No exceptions. Not only do you have to make this choice, but it is a decision that will affect all the decisions you will ever make. We, each of us individually, have to choose the god (God) we are going to serve. In addition, we get to choose any one we want because small "g" gods can't make us serve them and as surprising as it may seem, the big "G" (one, true living) God chooses not to make us. We have a choice to serve him or not.

The Old Testament people of God had to make this same choice and Joshua tells them so in his final speech. You may want to take a few minutes to read Joshua 24:14-15 and consider the choices presented to the Israelites at this point. Basically, Joshua is asking, "Who are you going to serve?" While we are not sure exactly which specific gods Joshua had in mind when he references "the gods your ancestors served on the other side of the River" or "the gods of the Amorites in whose land you live," the Israelite people would have

known. What we do know from history is that they had many false
gods to choose from in this ancient cultural reality. They would
have been able to name at least eight major false deity options:
Asheroth, Baal, Chemosh, Dagon, Egyptian gods (of which there
were 40 named), The Golden Calf, Marduk, and Milcom.

Fast forward 1,400 years and Jesus (remember he shares the
same Hebrew name Joshua which means "God saves") comes with
the same. His claims are remarkable: "I am God. I am the son of
God. I am the promised one to come. I have come in the flesh to
save you from your sins, but I'm not going to force you to follow
me." He left those he spoke to, and those of us who know him all
these years later, with a choice to believe or not to believe who he
was and who he said he was. A conversation Jesus had with Peter
helps clarify exactly what we are choosing when we choose Jesus.
Matthew's gospel tells us that one day as Jesus was hanging with
his followers; he asked them who people thought he was. They
answered that some thought he was Elijah or some other prophet
come back to life from the Old Testament days. Then he asked,
"Who do you say that I am?" The answer given by Peter revealed a
choice he had made. He had heard all that Jesus said and watched
all that he had done, and he was choosing Jesus as indicated in
this statement that we call the "good confession:" "You are the
Christ, the son of the living God" he said in Matthew 16:16. Jesus
commended him for his choice.

Two thousand years from that confession, we still hear that
good confession when people choose to follow Jesus. Before
baptisms, we have people confess their choice of Jesus. We could
say, "Who do you choose?" And they could respond, "I choose Jesus
as Lord." It's the same as the saying we have them repeat. "I believe
that Jesus is the Christ, the son of the living God. And I accept
(choose) him as both my Lord and Savior."

Two quick observations about Joshua's boldly stated choice:
First, "choose this day" indicates that there is only one time you can

choose to follow God – today. Yesterday is over, can't be changed, and tomorrow is not promised, so all we have is today. For Christ followers, there is an initial day we confess our faith in Christ, but there is also a daily choice to obey and follow him. Second, this is personal. Joshua as the leader of his house speaks for them, but first, he speaks for himself ("as for me"). Faith in Christ is not something your parents, your friends, or your pastor can choose for you; you must choose for yourself.

In the end, the people decided, "…we also will serve the Lord, for he is our God (v. 18)".

And when Joshua tried to dissuade them noting their rebellious nature, they declared their choice emphatically, "No, but we will serve the Lord (vs. 24)." We know who Joshua chose and we know who the children of Israel chose in this moment. The question remaining is "who will you choose?" Take some time in the space below to confess your belief and choice to follow Jesus.

If you're a Christ follower, you may have never expressed who you think Jesus is in this manner but let me encourage you to answer these questions. Who do you believe Jesus to be? What is your choice about Him? Make an "as for me…" statement and share it with someone else. If you have never made the choice to follow Jesus before, let me encourage you to choose him now. If you have questions, talk to your pastor, leader, or parent today. As always, be sure to refer to the appropriate group study in the pages below for further spiritual experiences for you and your group.

Day 8 - Choose

DAY 9 - CHOSEN PEOPLE

Deuteronomy 7:6&7

"For you are a people holy to the Lord your God. The Lord your God has chosen you to be a people for his treasured possession, out of all the peoples who are on the face of the earth. It was not because you were more in number than any other people that the Lord set his love on you and chose you, for you were the fewest of all peoples..."

There is an old playground ritual of picking teams (an exercise in value really) that most of us have experienced. Here's how it works. Two captains, usually of equal ability, are appointed to choose teams, the idea being that this will make for a fairly balanced competition. So the selection begins with all who wish to play standing in a line, quietly hoping that someone will choose them to be on his team. The captains are trying to select the best. The participants hope to hear their name and not be the last one picked. One by one, name by name, the teams are formed. Everyone has been chosen from the first to the last.

It is hard to imagine standing on an eternal cosmic playground with billions of others as the God of the universe selects those he wants to be on his team. Questions would flood our minds. Will he pick me? Does he see anything in me? Can I offer anything of value to him? Does he want me to join him? Is it possible that I could be a part of his victory plan? Well, we may never line up before the King of Heaven and be chosen, but I can tell you with certainty that he has chosen us. And, our story of being chosen begins with the Hebrew people and the scriptures from Deuteronomy above.

God made a promise to Abraham and his descendants and Moses confirms it in these verses. The Lord God had chosen the people of Israel. The word "chosen" has the idea of an eternal and original decision. God decided "before the foundation of the world" (Ephesians 1:4) that these offspring of Abraham, Isaac and Jacob would be his. And, he didn't just choose them; he loved them as a "treasured possession." This word (seg ul la' in Hebrew) is used to talk of wealth, and at its root means "to shut up." This means that God sees the people he has chosen with great value, like a valued possession a rich person might put in a safe to make sure it is not lost. God has chosen and values his people greatly.

Okay, that's great, but what does this idea of being chosen have to do with those of us who are not Jewish by race? Well, God's choosing of Abraham and his descendants, the children of Israel, is also a choosing of a bigger spiritual family through Jesus Christ. By faith in Christ, Christians "are Abraham's offspring and heirs according to the promise" (Galatians 3:29). Back to that verse in Ephesians, "…even as he chose us *in him [Christ]*" (Italics mine). This is why the apostle Peter confidently uses words from today's verses to describe the Christians in the first century who were also the people of God. "But you are a **chosen** race, a royal priesthood, a holy nation, a people for **his own possession**, that you may proclaim the excellencies of him who called you out of darkness into his marvelous light" (I Peter 2:9). Through Jesus, we have been chosen by God and this changes everything in each of our respective stories. Briefly, let's consider:

We are not chosen because we are good. The world we live in chooses us based on any number of traits, abilities, or success we have. And the Old Testament people of God may have thought

God chose them because they were great, but God didn't choose them because they were the biggest nation. In fact, early on their population was only 70 people living in Egypt (Exodus 1:5). God simply decided Abraham was his guy and Abraham's descendants were his people for accomplishing his will on earth. There was never a time in the history of the people of God, where any of them could declare that they were God's people because they earned it or deserved it. This is a huge lesson for those of us who are chosen through Jesus Christ. We have not and cannot earn his love. There is nothing we could ever do to impress God enough for him to choose us. Many of us have spent our entire lives trying to impress parents, teachers, coaches, peers, and people who don't even know us personally. We have tried to look good, win, succeed, advance, and be known all our lives, and yet all of us have been rejected (not chosen) more than we would like to admit. Stop trying to impress those who reject you. The one you can't impress has chosen you.

We are valuable because we are treasured. This choosing also changes each of our lives because God's treasuring makes us valuable. We spend much of our lives wondering if we matter. Does anyone need us? Do we have purpose? The problem is we are looking to other imperfect and unsure people for confirmation that we are valuable. In addition, many of us have been told on many different fronts that we don't really amount to much. But, today's teaching tells us that we have value because God treasures us. Everyone in Christ matters because God has placed our value at a very high price – the death of his Son Jesus. You are that valuable!

We are set apart because we have been chosen. Since we are chosen, we are holy. That means we set apart our lives, our dreams, our hopes, our resources, our relationships for him. He has chosen us, but he has chosen us to be set apart for him. Spend some time thinking, and maybe writing down a few thoughts about your being chosen because in eternity past, when you wondered if you would be picked, God called your name.

DAY 10 - CHOOSE WISELY

Deuteronomy 30:19&20

"I call heaven and earth to witness against you today, that I have set before you life and death, blessing and curse. Therefore choose life that you and your offspring may live, loving the Lord your God, obeying his voice and holding fast to him, for he is your life and length of days..."

You may recall the famous scene from "Indiana Jones and the Last Crusade," in which Harrison Ford's character is searching for the Holy Grail (drinking cup) of Jesus. Following clues, he makes his way through a series of obstacles to a cave where a table holding a large variety of drinking vessels is guarded by a knight. Soon after he arrives, his enemy Marcus Brody enters the cave hoping to procure the life-giving cup before Indy does. He asks the knight, "Which one is it?" The knight replies to him, "You must choose. But choose wisely, as the true grail will bring you life, and the false grail will take it from you." Brody ponders his decision, and eventually is convinced by his accomplice Dr. Elsa to choose a jeweled one. Cautiously, he dips this cup in the water and pressing it to his lips takes a drink. Immediately he melts away. At this, the knight stoically comments, "He chose poorly."

Near the end of his life, Moses (like our guy Joshua) called the people of Israel together so that he could give them some final words as their trusted leader. He too read the entirety of the law – "every blessing and every curse" in the audience of the whole nation. Moses also called some unlikely witnesses to the stand: "heaven and earth." But, unlike Joshua, Moses doesn't present the choice to follow as an option (i.e. "Choose whom you will serve"). He realizes that they have an option, and he knows all too well their tendency to choose poorly, but to him a decision for God and his ways can be summed up in a two-word encouragement: choose life.

Remember in yesterday's reading, we said that God chose us as his people? Well, the "choose" word there is the same "choose" word Moses uses here. In other words, he is saying that as God made an eternally past determination to love us, we can make an earthly and human determination to love and obey him. And, in this one choice to follow him, we find life. It really is that simple. To choose God and his way is to choose life. There is no clearer picture of this literal reality than a scene at the beginning of human history that took place a garden paradise long lost. The scene is of a woman, Eve by name, standing dangerously close to a tree whose fruit God had clearly forbidden. However, a serpent slithers in the background deceitfully luring her into the fruit's advantages. She has to choose whom she will believe. God was clear: "...the day you eat of it, you will surely die" (Genesis 2:17). Satan straight up lied: "You will not surely die" (Genesis 3:4). In that moment, she literally had a life and death decision. What would she do? I find myself reading this story thinking, "Don't do it Eve. Choose life!" She chose poorly.

What a terrible decision. What was she thinking? If you and I had been there at the tree instead of Adam and Eve, knowing what we now know, we would have walked away right? Probably not. We may never stand before a tree that God has assigned rules to, but what if we visited some other trees in the garden of life God has placed us in? Consider the choices we are giving in these prominent human trees.

The tree of sexuality. God's good life offer: "I have given you the pleasure of sex to be enjoyed within the lifetime commitment of marriage between a man and a woman to make them one and to create a nurturing environment for their children." Satan's lie: "Sex can define you. Sex is an activity for fun and every person has the right to participate and express their sexuality as they wish." Choose life.

The tree of materialism. God's good life offer: "I have blessed you with food and drink to sustain you, clothes to cover and protect you, and possessions to sustain you from day to day. Be generous with others as I have been with you." Satan's lie: "Accumulation of money and goods will make you happy and give you security for a lifetime of pleasure. Make more. Keep more. Fall in love with your riches." Choose life.

The tree of trust. God's good life offer: "Trust me in the hard times, the long stretches when you wish things were different; keep asking, seeking, and knocking. I will never leave you. Keep following me. I'm the way." Satan's lie: "When God seems far, turn to the gods of pleasure, drunkenness, fear, and worry. Try harder. Have it your way. Trust your feelings." Choose life.

The tree of words. God's good life offer: "I have given the Living Word and I have given you words. With them, you can heal, encourage, comfort, and bless. This is what I have done with my Word. Do the same to those around you." Satan's lie: "Curse, gossip, lie, slander, judge, and criticize before someone else does the same to you. Always have the first and last word."

The tree of relationships. God's good offer: "Be great by being servant of all. Be first by going last. Consider other's needs before your own. Do unto others as you would have done to you. Love others as I have loved you." Satan's lie: "Hang around others who build you up, make you look good, will do what you say. Use others to insure your own pleasure, happiness, and success."

Of course, there are other trees. Maybe you can spend some

time identifying and journaling about one of the trees above or another where you feel the greatest temptation. Ultimately, the tree doesn't matter; it is the voice we decide we will listen to. When we choose to listen to God and his life-giving commands, we choose life both now and forever more. But, for those who insist on listening to Satan's lies a destiny of an eternally painful existence separated from God. And what will be the testimony about those tragic souls? They chose poorly. Choose wisely.

DAY 11 - DO NOT CHOOSE

Proverbs 3:31

"Do not envy a man of violence and do not choose any of his ways"

At first glance, this scripture may seem to be an unnecessary reminder for those of us who desire to experience Jesus in our everyday lives. When Solomon first penned these words 3,000 years ago, one might well have responded, "Thank you, captain obvious." Of course, don't choose the violent way. We people of God should never choose the ways of someone who is blatantly opposed to God. Yet, culture (both then and now) seems to elevate those who humanly "succeed" in a way that tempts Christ-followers to subtly choose their ways.

Our verse for today specifically refers to being envious of a "man of violence" and you might be wondering why anyone would envy that guy. Why would I want to follow a guy who is prone to harming others? Well in the biblical world, kings, generals, and gladiators often became famous by treachery, cruelty, and murder. If you don't believe it, just read through the books of I Kings and II Kings. Like Old Testament mobsters, most of the kings during this period of history ruled through identifying, terrorizing, and killing their enemies. But as wicked as these kings were, the poor and upright often saw the results (rich palaces, authoritative power, and luxurious lifestyle) as something to be envied. This verse warns against choosing their ways; no matter how good of a life their ways seem to deliver.

But, violent men aren't the only sinners whose ways the godly are sometimes prone to choose. This is why the book of Psalms opens with a warning for the godly not to be influenced by the ungodly. "Blessed is the man who walks not in the counsel of the wicked, nor stands in the way of sinners, nor sits in the seat of scoffers" (Psalm 1:1). In other words, if you want to choose God's ways, you should avoid the company of those whose ways are not godly. Restated: "do not choose any of the ways of the wicked, sinners, or scoffers." It is safe to say, the Bible teaches us to stay away from following the ways of the world.

Again, most of us would agree wholeheartedly. "God's ways are right and I choose them, and the ways of this sin-saturated world are wrong, and I do not choose them." However, I have found in my life and the life of those I serve in the church, a very subtle choosing of the wrong ways of the world and its culture. I have identified at least three common ways we do this. Let's consider them together.

Do not choose the ways of celebrity.

We are tempted to choose the ways of celebrity. This is the culture of fame that is prevalent throughout the world today. Of course, our sports crazed culture makes celebrities of those who have great athletic ability. Others become celebrities because they are talented entertainers in music, movies, or comedy. Some become celebrities simply because they are attractive or rich. Still others achieve celebrity by working their way up the ladder of success to a title of prominence. No matter how one becomes a celebrity, they all have one thing in common. They have a voice.

We know celebrities because their lives are recorded, their words are quoted, and their opinions become headlines. But, consider this. Few are celebrities because they are leaders. Few are celebrities because they can articulate the best ways for social change. And fewer still are celebrities because they follow God. This means that we as Christians should keep them in the realm of their celebrity and not follow them because they are famous. For example, Lebron James may be the greatest basketball player in the world, and yes, he deserves to have a voice like any human being. However, his opinion is not necessarily right or even good because he can play basketball. Christians should guard against making celebrities role models because often the celebrities who entertain us will not lead us well.

Do not choose social media.

Most of us, even before you "follow," "favorite," or "quote" any one on social media, at least take a second to research who they are. This is because your endorsement of them is an endorsement of everything they say. There are a few red flags for those whose ways we should not follow. First, does their bio mention Jesus, God, or church? If not, their ways are probably not his ways. Second, do they have posts on their page that included suggestive photos or broad use of profanity? If so, don't choose to allow their ways to influence you. Third, do you find mean-spirited and hateful positions and language (are they haters?)? If so, you probably shouldn't choose exposure to their ways. Finally, are their posts about things that matter eternally, or are they shallow, worldly, and self-centered? If this is what their personal site is about, you will likely be choosing the wrong way by subjecting your mind and heart to it.

Do not choose the ways of non-Christian friends.

Don't get me wrong, Christians do and should have friends and acquaintances who are not followers of Jesus Christ. Otherwise, Jesus' call for us to be salt and light would be impossible for us to fulfill. Deep theology insight: you cannot flavor mashed potatoes without salt being shaken into them, and you cannot light the dark world unless you shine in it (see Matthew 5:13-16). However, there is a distinct danger for us as we mingle into this world we want to influence. On the one hand, our non-believing friends trust our voice, but we also come to love and trust their voice as well. This is fine when it comes to things like their opinion on favorite restaurants, sports teams, shared activities, doctors or schools, but not on spiritual life choices that require a Christ-following perspective. I have seen way too many Christians take the advice of their unbelieving friends on divorce, sexuality, depression, and finances. The bottom line is that when you need to make a moral or life decision, do not choose to listen to non-Christians. They simply will not give you guidance from the perspective that matters most.

Spend some time today on your journal pages identifying which of these three ways you are most prone to follow and how you can work at "choosing not to follow."

DAY 12 - SERVE SOMEONE

Luke 16:13

"No servant can serve two masters, for either he will hate the one and love the other, or he will be devoted to the one and despise the other. You cannot serve God and money."

In 1979, rocker Bob Dylan won a Grammy for Best Rock Vocal Performance by a male. What makes this song unique is the unsuspected theology from a guy not necessarily known for his spirituality. Nevertheless, the single "Gotta Serve Somebody" perfectly describes the teaching from today's Scripture. The profoundly black and white lyrics share a simple and eternal truth in the chorus: "But you're gonna have to serve somebody, yes. Indeed you're gonna have to serve somebody. Well, it may be the devil or it may be the Lord. But you're gonna have to serve somebody."

In the Roman-conquered world of the early first century during which Jesus' ministry took place, it is estimated that as many as one third of all people were slaves. This means that those who heard Jesus' first century sermon on serving thoroughly understood the slave-master relationship. Many of them were or had been slaves and served somebody. There were also those in his audience (the religious leaders known as Pharisees "lovers of money" according to Luke 16:14) who were likely slave owners. They understood being served. So it is that Jesus used this cultural reality to teach about serving and loyalty, servants and masters.

Jesus is saying that everyone is a servant.

Jesus would wholeheartedly agree with the lyrics of the song mentioned above. Everyone is a servant to something or someone. There are no exceptions. You're gonna have to serve somebody. Of course, this reality falls harshly on American ears aware that the evil of slavery is a part of our history. By God's will and movement, we no longer have a literal slave trade with cruel masters today. However, every American, regardless of skin color, background, social standing, or family origin is enslaved to something or someone.

For starters, most of us, have been (or still are) enslaved to sin. This is Jesus' take on the sin situation from John 8:34: "Truly, truly, I say to you, everyone who practices sin is a slave to sin." This means that sin, like a literal slave master, tells us what we have to do and we submit. In other words, there are no sins that give us true freedom. If you choose drugs, they will demand you do anything to keep taking them. If you choose to find your worth in sexuality, sex will drive you to do what you don't want to do. Become a slave to selfishness and your selfish desires will imprison you in a cell of loneliness. Declare success as your master, and it will drive you until you literally die trying. You get the point; the sins we choose to be loyal to, the physical desires and pleasures of this world, end up owning, mistreating, and destroying us.

Jesus is saying that you can't serve both.

The specific slave-master Jesus addresses in the context of our verse for the day is money. The word translated "money" here was translated "mammon" in some of our older English versions of the Bible. This was a transliteration of an old word the ancient

Chaldean culture used to express confidence in wealth and riches. Therefore, the Greek word, "mamonas" (the word Jesus actually spoke during this teaching) indicated a trust in tangible worldly wealth. In other words, I will enslave myself to money. "What money says, I will do. What the accumulation of money costs, I'll give. What financial security demands, I will sacrifice. I'm not in charge anymore; money is my master."

Jesus says plainly, you can serve money if you want to, but you can't serve God and money. Logically, serving two masters doesn't work because each master requires his will to be done by the servant. And, two masters would obviously have different desires and needs. Taking commands from two different masters would at the least be confusing and at the most be frustrating. It wouldn't take long before the demands and demeanor of one master would be seen as kinder. This would naturally sway the love and allegiance of the slave in that master's direction.

It's the same with God and money. God and money have two different economies. The goals of these two masters are completely opposite. The master money is the economy of the world. The goal is to get as much as you can. Make money. Earn money. Keep money. Save and spend money on yourself. Money has the appearance of being free, because with it you can buy things, accumulate things, and live comfortably. However, all of these things can be gone in a moment. Money can be stolen or lost. Tragedy can cost everything you've saved. Worse yet, when you die, all these things accumulated are no longer yours. Or, as the old money saying goes, "you can't take it with you."

God's economy on the other hand places a very low value on money and the things money can buy. In fact, God has all the wealth in the world, so money doesn't impress him and in fact, is pretty worthless. With God as master, you "invest" in your soul and focus on your relationship with Jesus, a free gift he has given all who accept him. The great thing about this economy is that you are granted the eternal riches of God and it can never be taken away. This means that the only true freedom we can find is to willingly be servants to the One who freed us from sin so that we could choose him.

So who is your master? Reflect on that question today. After all, as the song...I mean Jesus says, "You gotta serve somebody."

DAY 13 - COUNT THE COST
Luke 14:27&28

"Whoever does not bear his own cross and come after me cannot be my disciple. For which of you, desiring to build a tower, does not first sit down and count the cost, whether he has enough to complete it?"

Nearly thirty years ago I went on my first mission trip to the Dominican Republic with an organization called Christ in Youth to hold a student conference. The group was primarily made up of youth pastors and we were excited to be a part of translating the conference from the previous summer in the States into the culture of our Dominican brothers and sisters. This, of course, meant bi-lingual counterparts to translate our English lessons, sermons, and conversations into Spanish. Along the way, we learned (and often butchered to the delight of our hosts) some Spanish words and phrases.

We learned important phrases for the conference like "Dios te bendiga" which means, "God bless you," "Como se llama?" to ask a student's name, and "Cuantos anos tienes?" to inquire of their age. These phrases, combined with the student's English, hand gestures, and facial expressions helped us communicate and form bonds with these students we grew to love. But, it was the experience of heading to a market on the last day of our trip that taught me the most important phrase for an American tourist in a Spanish speaking culture. "Cuanto es?" is the question necessary for determining whether you will buy any number of items from the merchants trying to sell their wares. Before you buy, you must count the cost. So you ask, "How much is it?"

The verse for the day comes from something Jesus said while his popularity was rising and many were following him. They liked his teaching and authority. They thrilled at his miracle healing. They warmed to his care for the sick and the poor. They didn't mind it when he miraculously provided lunch for everyone. No wonder "...great crowds accompanied him" (Luke 14:25)! At this point in his ministry, Jesus' popularity and poll numbers were up. He was the greatest show in Israel. But, Jesus didn't come to win popularity contests and break attendance records; he came to make disciples and following Jesus isn't free. So he teaches this crowd about the cost of discipleship. He says, "Before you follow me, you should first ask 'how much is it?'" In other words, count the cost.

He used two first century illustrations to make this point. First, he talks about how embarrassing it would be if a man began to build a tower (probably a building on the edge of one's farm or vineyard) and was not able to complete it because of shortage of funds. A half-built tower is not very useful, but it sure is obvious. Second, he speaks of a king going to war and his crucial assessment of power when it comes to challenging an advancing enemy. It would be foolish (not to mention deadly) to rush into war without thinking through the numbers. And so Jesus says to "count," a Greek word meaning "to add up or calculate." And in this teaching, he mentions three calculations every Christ follower needs to make before choosing to be his disciple. Let's consider them with three questions.

Is following Jesus worth all of my relationships? Jesus opens this entire teaching with the less-than-attractional, "If anyone comes to me and does not hate his own father and mother and wife and children and brothers and sisters…he cannot be my disciple" (Luke 14:26). To our English-speaking ears, Jesus couldn't have spoken harsher words, but in the first century Jewish idiom the word "hate" could have the meaning of "love less." Obviously, Jesus never asks us to hate anyone, so we should understand Jesus to be saying that if we want to follow him, our relationships have to be secondary to him. Remember, he's not demanding or angry, he's just teaching about how much it costs to follow.

Think through your relationships right now. Are any of them taking precedence over your relationship with Jesus? Are you a young adult still trying to please your parents, following their desires for your career, education, and financial future instead of listening to His calling for your life? Are you a parent, who puts your children's activities ahead of church participation? Are you a single who is allowing a dating relationship to pull you away or distract you from your walk with Jesus? Are you (at any life stage) allowing your acceptance among peers and friends to weaken your purity and commitment to Christ?

Is following Jesus worth all my possessions? Jesus also caps this teaching with the all-inclusive verse, "So therefore, any one of you who does not renounce all that he has cannot be my disciple" (Luke 14:33). In other words, if there is anything in your life that holds more value than Jesus does, you can't follow him. This is not necessarily a call to sell all of your possessions and take a vow of poverty. I say, "not necessarily" because some indeed are called to this kind of sacrifice. However, it is a call to steward all that we have (money, possessions, and comforts) in such a way that it never becomes more important than Jesus does.

The best way to keep Jesus in the forefront of your possessions is to consistently and regularly give more in the name of Jesus and for his kingdom. This is why regular giving to your church, missionaries and church organizations is crucial for Christ-followers. The more we give, the less important earthly treasures become as we invest in God's eternal kingdom. Is Jesus worth all that you have? You can test this by giving something away in his name. Go ahead. Try it.

Is following Jesus worth all that I am? Finally, Jesus paints a vivid picture of cost by talking to these crowds about bearing their cross. The cross meant one thing and one thing only in Jesus' day. It meant death. To carry a cross meant you were on your way to be executed (crucified, they called it). In other words, following Jesus will cost you your life. As much as I'd like to tell you this is figurative, it's not. Historically millions have literally given their lives for their faith in Christ and increasingly our culture is filled with murders that are anti-Christian. Still, the picture of carrying a cross is Jesus' way of saying we must die daily to our selves. Or, as Paul would later write, "...present your bodies as a living sacrifice..." (Romans 12:1). Is the one who carried his cross for you worth carrying a cross for?

We don't really know the crowd's reaction that day, but I'll bet Jesus' speech caused many to stop and think. Many likely abandoned him at this point. What about you? Take a few minutes today to calculate in the journal pages provided about your relationships, possessions, and life. If you had to give them all up for Jesus, is He worth it? Of course, the church answer is "yes;" most would never say, "Jesus costs too much." But, he does cost a lot, so count the cost.

DAY 14 - CHOOSE TO LOSE

Mark 8:34

"And calling the crowd to him with his disciples, he said to them, 'If anyone would come after me, let him take up his cross and follow me. For whoever would save his life will lose it, but whoever loses his life for my sake and the gospel's will save it. For what does it profit a man to gain the whole world and forfeit his soul?'"

My good friend, Cal Jernigan, leads a thriving church in Phoenix, Arizona whose logo, like that of many churches, includes an image of the cross. What's striking about this cross, however, is that it's not standing upright with cross beams extending left and right, rather the cross on their logo is laying on its side. This is the result of a happy accident that now has great meaning for the congregation. The cross was originally designed to stand upright in a niche high above the stage in the front of the original auditorium, making it the focal point of the worship center. However, a design oversight meant that the cross was too big to fit into the intended space. The solution? Lay the cross horizontally, on its side. Perfect fit… and perfect picture.

What began as a construction gaff has become a meaningful symbol to the people of Central Christian Church for following Christ in two ways. First, it represents the finished work of Jesus on the cross. He bore the cross. He was crucified for our sins on the cross. Ultimately, he lay the cross down, having conquered the death and sin it represented. Jesus is done with the cross! What a powerful message. The second symbol of "the cross on its side" is the constant reminder that we are called to take up the cross and bear it in the name of Christ. This image of the cross, ready to be lifted, is an inspiration to me every time I see it and is exactly what today's verse is all about.

As we discussed in yesterday's study from Luke 14, taking up the cross is part of the Jesus following life (i.e. "Whoever does not bear his own cross...cannot be my disciple.") We mentioned that to bear the cross signifies death, but what are the implications of this willingness to die? Thankfully, we have a perfect "cross-bearing" example in Jesus as beautifully outlined for us by the apostle Paul in Philippians Chapter Two. If we look closely at the cross of Christ, we get a picture of what "our cross to bear" looks like.

Choose to lose yourself.

The cross you bear is not about you. To carry a cross is to get over oneself. To follow Christ is to give up who we are in the same way that Jesus gave up who he was. Philippians 2:6 & 7 says, "...though he was in the form of God, did not consider equality with God a thing to be grasped, but emptied himself, by taking the form of a servant, being born in the likeness of men." You cannot bear the cross and stay the same. You have to morph into something different. This literally is what Jesus did to change "forms" from God to human – he morphed (from the Greek "morphe)." People who bear a cross don't focus on themselves, their goals, or their comfort. The cross is uncomfortable. People who choose to carry an instrument of impending death don't complain when things get hard or don't go their way. Cross bearers don't look glamorous, famous, popular, successful, or put together. By getting under the cross, they have gotten over themselves.

If this sounds hard, it is. But consider the change Jesus made. He was God, one with the Father. He was eternal, always existing. He had absolute authority, nothing to fear. He was in perfect harmony, joy, and fellowship with the Holy Trinity. Yet he willingly chose to lose his "Godness" by emptying himself into a human body. Knowing what we know about humans and what we can conceive about God, there has never been a greater step down than when Jesus went from being God to being man. We are called to do the same.

Choose to lose yourself for the sake of others.

The cross you bear is best understood in the context of serving others. The cross is about those around you. Again, the example of Jesus comes from Paul's encouragement to "Do nothing from selfish ambition or conceit, but in humility count others more significant than yourselves. Let each look not only to his own interests, but also to the interests of others" (Philippians 2:3&4).

We often joke that our spouse, children, friend, or neighbor is "our cross to bear," but it is no joke. As cross bearers everyone around us is our cross to bear. We lose ourselves to serve others. In Jesus, the needs and interests of everyone in our life takes precedence over ours. What would it look like if you looked first after your spouse's needs? What would happen if students asked, "How can I help mom and dad today?" What would it mean for classmates to embrace and include the kids who are different and ridiculed? How could we change the workplace, our town, and this culture if we set out each day to put someone else's needs ahead of ours? This kind of humility is exactly what Jesus did when "… he humbled himself by becoming obedient to the point of death, even death on a cross" (Philippians 2:9). He didn't die for his own interest, but for ours.

Choose to lose your life to gain it.

The famous missionary, Jim Elliot, who was killed by the indigenous South American tribe he was attempting to reach with the gospel, was credited with saying, "He is no fool who gives what he cannot keep to gain what he cannot lose." This is the eternal perspective and attitude Jesus is encouraging in his followers. Taking up the cross is a sign that one is willing to give up everything the world has to offer, even if it means dying for the Name like Elliot did. But the result is eternal life with Jesus.

This is the result of Jesus' cross bearing as well. His death was only temporary. "Therefore God has highly exalted him and bestowed on him the name that is above every name…" (Philippians 2:9). In the same way, our death on earth is only temporary and by his resurrection we too will rise to live a new life and eternal life. In other words when we choose to lose, we gain.

DAY 15 - REPENT

Joshua 24:23&24

"Then put away the foreign gods that are among you, and incline your heart to the Lord, the God of Israel." And, the people said to Joshua, "the Lord our God we will serve, and his voice we will obey."

What are the things you truly value? Don't give me your church answer yet. I am talking about tangible possessions that all of us have around our home, office, storage facility, or in our safe. Maybe your treasure is some sort of family heirloom - grandpa's old watch, grandma's wedding ring, some of mom's good China, or one of your children's art projects. I have always communicated to my grown sons that our family photos and the journals I have kept throughout most of my adult life are all that I truly value. However, truth be told, there are some earthly possessions that I value because they have real monetary value: wedding rings and jewelry, flat screen televisions and cars, estate wills and life insurance policies. I have a friend who recently discovered upon his mother's passing that she had a tube sock full of collectible coins in a safety deposit box that the family was unaware of. What are the things you have hidden away, displayed, or protected that mean a lot to you?

Your answer to this question is important because the things we value have the potential to steal our hearts from God. This is Joshua's concern for the Israelites who have just confirmed that they choose God while simultaneously being in possession of "foreign gods" (probably idols - miniature replicas of different deities) even as he preaches. During his ministry on earth, Jesus taught, "you cannot serve two masters" (Matthew 6:24) and "... where your treasure is, there your heart will be also." (Matthew 6:21). We may not actually sing songs of praise and worship toward our "idols" of possession and we may not pray and offer sacrifices to them. I have never heard anyone declare loyalty and trust in a car or favorite piece of furniture, but that doesn't mean we aren't idolaters. Anything that steals attention, resources, time, or passion away from God is an idol that can potentially get in the way of following him.

What's the answer? Though Joshua doesn't actually use the church term, his prescription is a word you may have heard before - "repentance." This word (metanoia in Greek) is used extensively in the early church writings and literally means "to change the mind." Put into practice, this changing of mind results in turning from the direction one is heading and going the opposite way. A spiritual kind of about-face. Repentance is willfully turning (put away) from whatever idols we value and heading intentionally in God's direction (incline your heart to the Lord).

Repentance begins by putting something away. The Hebrew word translated into English as "put away" is the word "sur" and it means literally to turn aside or away. For Israel, this means not only throwing their false divinity statues out with the trash, but also turning away from the idolatrous practices of their culture. Joshua is calling them to put away anything that takes the place of the Lord God. For us, this first step to repenting is also a turning away from the false gods of self – our desires, our possessions, and our pride. This is not easy because unlike our ancient spiritual relatives, our idols are not always visible and tangible. We sometimes have become so conformed to the Canaan we live in that we are completely unaware of our idolatry. This idolatry expresses itself in many forms but there are three "foreign gods" that I have identified that we as Christians need to put away.

The idol of relationship. A dangerous idol for many of us is the false god of relationship. This form of idolatry is one that elevates any relationship (even good ones) into an unhealthy level of service, compromise, or priority. This form of idolatry can be expressed when parents prioritize their children's needs and activities over church attendance, spending, or spiritual nurture. It can express itself in a dating relationship with a non-believer that compromises commitment to God's standards for sexuality. Relational idolatry is often expressed in a desire to please a friend and seek their approval above all. I could go on, but the question is, "Are there relationships in your life that are more important to you than God?"

The idol of materialism. Another idol of our culture is a bit more obvious: the idol of materialism. This is easier to identify because it's so obvious, but not so easy to walk away from. Our challenge is that the culture makes pseudo-god promises through endless marketing that claims newer technology, hipper clothes, and cooler cars will bring us happiness and contentment. It's easy to see that even Christians are caught up in this belief because we spend just as much money on goods and services as non-Christians. Here's the question, "Do you seek happiness and worth in the buying and accumulation of stuff?"

The idol of busyness. Finally, the evil god called busyness. This is more elusive than just about any other god because our technological advances allow us to accomplish more than ever before. We stack so many events into our days and weeks, all the while bragging about our ability to multi-task. What I've found in my life is that multi-tasking is the ability to be mediocre in several endeavors at one time. The result is a lack of focus and grounding;

a constant rushing around; perpetual exhaustion; a deep desire for rest. Is this how you feel? You may be worshiping the foreign god of busyness. Two other questions to consider: "does your current pace of life produce fruit or exhaustion?" And, "Is your current pace of life sustainable?"

The second part of Joshua's challenge is to "incline" your heart to the Lord. Repentance calls us not only to turn from that which is false and dead, but also to turn to the living God with all our heart. The word "incline" is the Hebrew word "na tah" which could be translated "to stretch out or extend." In other words, to repent we have to stretch our hearts toward God – to replace our old gods with the ONE who is truly worthy and who can fulfill our deepest soul longings. As we continually extend our whole hearts in his direction, he will change us from within.

Incline your heart to God and you will find relationship in his perfect love that will put all other relationships into proper perspective.

Incline your heart to God and you will find meaning not in possessions, but in things eternal and as the old hymn says, "the things of earth will grow strangely dim."

Incline your heart to God and you will find rest for your soul that will allow you to take life at a reasonable and sustainable pace as you learn to live with him and for him.

It is not enough to simply articulate that we choose Jesus. At some point, the declaration of who or what we are going to serve must lead to actions that support that choice. So what are you going to do? Take some time to write down the idols in your life that get in the way of relationship with Jesus and some steps you can take to put them away. In addition, what are some ways you can incline your heart to Him? Be sure to refer to the appropriate groups study in the pages below for further spiritual experiences for you and your group.

DAY 16 - ENOUGH

Ezekiel 45:9

---

*"Thus says the Lord God: Enough, O princes of Israel! Put away
violence and oppression, and execute justice and righteousness."*

Two brothers are wrestling. Why? Because they are boys
and there is something hard wired into the male DNA that
compels them to test their strength against one another. So
wrestling happens in a house with boys and I might add, sisters
are often drawn into this exercise of strength. Most often it was
pretty innocent, almost playful – what my grandma used to call
"horseplay" or "rough housing." However, these matches that began
competitively with laughing, challenging, and rolling around on
the floor usually devolved into an exercise of name-calling, pain,
and general destruction. As a father, I usually tolerated these games
at first. In fact, up until Mikey and Caleb became young adults, I
would often jump in to show them that papa bear still had it.

So against mom's better judgment, I would go on reading,
watching T.V., or whatever I was doing, with the sounds of "boys
being boys" in the background. This continued until one of three
things ended the fun (and yes, 100% of them ended in one of these
ways in our house). The first way to stop a fight was physical harm.
One of the boys would chip a tooth, start bleeding, or start crying

and that was it. Game over. The second way for the fun to come to an end was a broken lamp, a hole in the wall, knocking over furniture, or some other damage to the home. This is where mom usually declared a truce with a loud and passionate, "Boys! Stop it!"

The final way the wrestling ended was the least predictable because it had to do with the tolerance and patience of dad (in this case, me.) It could be that the annoyance of the ever- increasing yelling and thuds on the floor had reached the point of being too bothersome. Sometimes it was an intuition that things were getting a little out of hand and soon someone would be hurt, or something would be broken (see above). Whatever it was, when I had had enough, I usually ended it all with an authoritative "Knock it off!," or as God says in our verse for the day, "Enough!" This is God's version of the old parent line, "I've had it up to here" with your sin.

God hates sin. The differences between me (as dad) and the Lord God (as Heavenly Father) are myriad, but one obvious difference I'll point out here is that our Eternal Dad never thinks sin is okay. This is because he personifies the two words that he calls us to in the verse for the day. He is a perfect combination of "justice" (the Hebrew word "mish pat" that means to judge) and righteousness ("tsed a ka') whose root literally means "to do or be right." In other words, there is never a time when God does something that is not fair or right. This means there is never a time when God tolerates our sin. To be clear, all of us (yes, even you) are prone to sin and have things in our lives that are either unfair, not right, or both. Take a moment today in the journal space provided to think through some sins (even "small" ones like impatience in traffic, selfishness with your family, or judging others by their looks) that you have in your life.

God knows your sin. Whatever sins you struggle with, have written down, or have confessed in prayer to God, don't expect him to be surprised when you tell him. He knows our sin. He knew Adam and Eve ate the fruit. He knew King David had committed adultery. And he knows every wrong word, thought, and motive of ours. In our complacency and selfishness, we often convince ourselves that we're getting away with something, but we're not. We can fool a lot of people, even those closest to us, but God sees every wrong we do. In our reading today, God had been watching those in authority positions in Israel ("princes") and knew that they were being violent and oppressive towards those they were supposed to be serving. He was fully aware that these leaders were cheating poor people by using false measurements, confiscating the property of the weak, and physically abusing those who weren't compliant. If you are in a person of authority, take note. God is especially displeased when our sin harms those he has entrusted to our care. But whether you are a leader or not, God knows your sin.

God has a boiling point. Eventually our sins reach a boiling point with God. I've said many times in sermons if God punished us every time we sinned, we'd all be walking wounded. For some reason, he doesn't lash out immediately at every misdeed, transgression, or rebellion against him. Why? Well, he's the most patient and merciful dad there is. The Psalmist says, "The Lord is gracious and merciful, slow to anger and abounding in steadfast love" (Psalm 145:8). The apostle Peter also gives us insight into why God hasn't yet said "enough" and ended it all, "The Lord... is patient toward you, not wishing that any should perish, but that all should reach repentance" (I Peter 3:9.) He goes on in verse 10: "But the day of the Lord will come like a thief, and then the heavens will pass away with a roar, and the heavenly bodies will be burned up and dissolved, and the earth and the works that are done on it will be exposed."

My advice? Repent. It's the word we're talking about this week, and if we are going to truly be Christ followers, we are going to have to get good at repenting. There are three repentance steps that should be the reflexive prayer of the saints. 1. Tell God he's right. 2. Tell God you're wrong. 3. Tell him you desire to "put away" your sins. Don't be afraid. Our God always (always!) accepts the sincere repentance of his children. Because of his justice and righteousness, and Jesus' work on the cross, our repentance makes us righteous. "If we confess our sins, he is faithful and just to forgive us our sins, and cleanse us from all unrighteousness" (I John 1:9.)

Sin, like household wrestling matches, is either going to end in repentance or in pain and general destruction. The goal is to keep from hearing our Eternal Dad yelling, "Enough!" Lord, give us the strength to repent before someone gets hurt.

DAY 17 - TORN
Joel 2:12&13

"'Yet even now,' declares the Lord, 'return to me with all your heart, with fasting, with weeping, and with mourning; and rend your hearts and not your garments.' Return to the Lord your God, for he is gracious and merciful, slow to anger, and abounding in steadfast love; and he relents over disaster."

In the book of Jonah, we find the story of one of the most unlikely "repenters" in the Bible. After the prophet Jonah initially flees and comes to his senses in the belly of the whale, he finally fulfills his God-given assignment by going to preach to the city of Nineveh. It is likely the most effective sermon ever preached, because with just eight words ("Yet forty days, and Nineveh shall be overthrown!" [Jonah 3:4]), the entire city repented. Even the number one citizen, the king of Nineveh, joined in! In the ancient tradition of biblical times, he displayed humility by discarding his royal robes and sitting in sackcloth and ashes. And when God saw that the whole city had humbled themselves, he forgave them and called off the destruction. But he didn't forgive them because of their outward display (i.e. sitting in sackcloth and ashes). He relented because they changed their hearts and turned to him.

There are many ways to express the deep sorrow and pain of

the human heart when calamity hits. Some show their pain by literally crying aloud and making a huge demonstration of their sorrow. We often see this display at a funeral. Others simply sit in the stunned silence of disbelief and are too numb to speak. In another display, the deep emotions can be shown through outbursts of anger, punching walls, or breaking things. I have personally witnessed this as a youth pastor in the passionate student world of break ups and broken hearts. Other times, people turn to numbing their pain, fears, and regrets through alcohol, food, shopping, or drugs. All of these outward displays indicate something that is happening in the heart.

This brings us to the reading from Joel today. Joel was an Old Testament prophet from the years 860-850 B.C. who evidently lived in or near Jerusalem in the tribal region of Judah. Context is important in understanding today's passage. Joel was the Lord's prophet during the 52-year reign of King Uzziah, who next to King Solomon was likely the most successful king to sit on the throne. During Uzziah's reign, there was relative peace, freedom of worship, and economic prosperity. Along with these was spiritual apathy. This is why Joel addresses much of this book to the elders, priests, and ministers of the altar.

They are following the prescribed spiritual activities but seem to be going through the motions, even when it comes to repentance. In Joel's prophecy, he references a locust attack of epic proportions. It seems that the Lord (as he often does with his people) had allowed an invasion of locusts to wake up his people. In their prosperity, they had become lukewarm in their serving and their worship of God, and now the locust invasion had thoroughly destroyed all of their crops and caused a severe famine (Joel 1:4). So, what does one do in the Bible times to show deep grief in times of harsh circumstances? What is the proper response if one wants to show God humility and sorrow for the sin of complacency?

The outward sign of repentance was to grab whatever garment

one was wearing at the neck and violently tear it as a sign of contrition. It is likely that in public worship at the temple, in the public market, and maybe even in the king's court, the leaders of Israel had dramatically torn their clothes in response to this plague as a demonstration of their repentance. The people may have been impressed with this show of contrition and followed along in this outward act of rending their garments (tailors must have done a booming business in these times). The problem with all this tearing of clothes is that it was just a show, an insincere going through the motions. But God was not impressed.

God was not impressed because there is more to repentance than just tearing your clothes. Repentance is a matter of the heart. True repentance occurs when one's heart is literally ripped with the realization of sin. True repentance is the result of a torn heart that is turning to God. True repentance comes from a heart that knows it is broken because it has sinned and fallen short of God's right way. True repentance is the returning of our hearts to the one who knows our hearts better than we do. Anyone can look repentant on the outside, but God sees the real intentions of the heart. So God says, "Return to me with all your heart" and "rend your hearts and not your garments."

King David also teaches us about repentance in Psalm 51 as he prays for God's forgiveness for his sin with Bathsheba. This included adultery, murder, and lying. "For you will not delight in sacrifice, or I would give it; you will not be pleased with a burnt offering. The sacrifices of God are a broken spirit; a broken and contrite heart, O God, you will not despise." So according to the Scriptures, it is possible to tear your clothes and sacrifice a burnt offering and not truly repent. Since we don't tear our clothes and make live sacrifices any more, our insincere repentance looks a little different. We must consider that it's possible to pray "Father forgive me," say "I'm sorry," or confess, "I'm a sinner," without truly repenting.

As you consider your repentance story, let these two questions guide your meditation, prayer, and journaling today.

Is my heart broken? When you consider your sin, does it break your heart that you have strayed so far from God's standards? Think through the sins you struggle with. If you can't think of any, you can start with pride and dishonesty. Do these sins you're aware of in your life truly make you sad? Do you regret them? Do they hurt your heart? If so, you are on the way to repentance.

Does my heart want to change? There is a difference between being sorry because you were caught and being sorry because you truly want forgiveness. One is "sorry" because you don't want to have to face the consequence of your sin; the other is "sorry" because you want another chance. Again, as you consider the sins in your life, do you truly want to change or do you just want God to overlook them?

Deal with your heart today…just you and God. After all, he is gracious, merciful, slow to anger, and abounding in love.

DAY 18 - BE BAPTIZED

Acts 2:37&38

"Now when they heard this they were cut to the heart, and said to Peter and the rest of the apostles, 'Brothers, what shall we do?' And Peter said to them, 'Repent and be baptized every one of you in the name of Jesus Christ for the forgiveness of your sins, and you will receive the gift of the Holy Spirit.'"

I was baptized when I was seven years old. Though many years have passed since then, I can still vividly recall the emotions, thoughts, fears, and even scenes from that warm July evening in Indianapolis. Our church always sang an "invitation hymn" – a song designed to allow people to make a decision for Christ at the end of each service. As I recall most services passed with no one coming down the aisle, but still we sang as the preacher waited down front. On this night, the arrangements had been made. At some point during the song, I would boldly step out into the aisle and walk slowly to the front where the preacher would welcome me with open arms. These literal and figurative steps of faith began the process for my baptism.

As the church continued to sing, I was led (accompanied by mom and dad) to the changing room that flanked the baptistery at the front of the sanctuary. There I changed into a white robe and when the music stopped I was directed down into the water to join the preacher from my youth, Dick Piper (couldn't make this up, that was his name). With tender seriousness, he helped me make the "good confession" publicly by asking me to repeat the words, "I believe that Jesus is the Christ, the son of the living God and my personal Lord and Savior." With that, he covered my nose with a handkerchief and laid me back into the water in the name of the Father, Son and Holy Spirit. As he lifted me out of the water, I heard the church singing the same song it always did when someone was baptized, "Now I Belong to Jesus..." and I went back to the changing room feeling as clean as I ever had before.

Baptism is an important 2,000-year-old Christian ritual that finds its origins on the very first day of the church. Actually, baptism predates Christianity going back into our Jewish heritage and the many cleansing and purification washings. Some Jewish sects (like the Essenes at Qumran) used baptism as a regular part of worship to symbolize spiritual as well as physical cleanliness. Baptism by immersion was the practice of the early church and fully captures the Greek word "baptidzo" that means, "to dunk, dip, or plunge." But it is more than just putting someone under the water. Baptism, like sacrifices and torn garments, is only an outward sign of a heart change. It is a picture of the death, burial, and resurrection of Jesus Christ. Dead and buried in the sin of our old selves we are raised to eternal life through the resurrecting power of Jesus. This is why repentance and baptism go hand in hand.

Biblically, baptism is seen to be pretty important. Jesus was baptized as an example. Every conversion story in the New Testament involved a baptism. In addition, the early church teachers saw baptism as a picture of the washing of our sin (Acts 22:16), a burial with Christ (Colossians 2:12), clothing ourselves with Christ (Galatians 3:27), and a part of our commission to make disciples (Matthew 28:19). But the act of going under the water is not complete without repentance. This is what Peter said when the church was born on Pentecost as we have already read in our verse today.

His famous "repent and be baptized" statement was the climax of a longer sermon in which he told the people that Jesus had come to save them, but they along with their leaders had rejected and killed him. What happens next is what we've been reading and journaling about for a couple of days now. The people are convicted. They are cut to the heart. They realize they have sinned, and they want to know how they can be saved from their wrongdoing. This movement of the heart is called repentance, and that's why the first word out of Peter's mouth is "repent." Baptism is important, but it doesn't mean anything without a faith decision from a repentant heart. Repentance is the Greek word "metanoia" that means literally "to change one's mind" but practically has the idea of turning around. In other words, to repent one must turn from their own way of thinking, and turn towards God.

I'm thankful my preacher understood this when I was a seven year old. The scariest part of my conversion story was not walking down the aisle in front of the whole church (although I remember being plenty scared.) The most intense part was meeting with my preacher so that he could make sure I was really ready to make Jesus my Lord. I remember him smiling across his large desk as my feet dangled from the chair across from him. Of course, he started with what I believed about Jesus, but I distinctly remember him asking me three questions that got me to the repentance part of my story. First, he asked if I understood what sin was and I told him it was when we do bad things that God doesn't like. Then he asked me if I sinned and if so what they were. I was embarrassed, but I admitted I did sin, and actually listed a few (things like lying to my parents and hitting my sister). Finally, he asked me what I thought about my sin. I told him that I was sorry for them and I didn't want to do them anymore. His grin gave it away; he knew I was ready for baptism because I had just repented.

Let me encourage you to spend some time reflecting on your story by recalling some of the details of your conversion experience. You may wish to do as I did above and write as much as you can remember about the day you were baptized. Here are some questions to help you. How old were you when you were baptized? Where were you baptized and who baptized you? What emotions can you recall from that day? What did you understand about repentance when you decided to follow Jesus? And what does your baptism mean to you now?

There is a good chance that many of you reading this chapter have never repented and been baptized. If so, think about what sins you know you need to turn from and tell Jesus you want to change. Then tell someone who you know is a Christ follower. Two things I know. You can have faith in Jesus because he has done all the work to forgive your sins. And if you're ready to repent and be baptized, we'd be honored to be a part of your story; just let us know.

DAY 19 - SAY IT

Ephesians 4:25 & 31

"Therefore, having put away falsehood, let each of you speak the truth with his neighbor, for we are members of one another....do not let the sun go down on your anger...Let the thief no longer steal...Let no corrupting talk come out of your mouths...let all bitterness and wrath and anger and clamor and slander be put away from you, along with all malice."

A small gathering of local pastors gathered for their annual retreat at the church camp they all supported. Each welcomed this two-day experience for it was a chance to be with others who understood the challenges of church leadership. It was a time of encouraging, praying, laughing, renewal, and bearing each other's burdens represented by their respective congregations. As each man arrived, they gathered for small talk and coffee in the lodge, the warmth of the fireplace cut the mountain chill. And then it happened. An unexpected retreat participant uneasily entered with his overnight bag. Uncomfortable greetings welcomed him.

Years before, this man was a legendary preacher in a big city with a thriving ministry. Unfortunately (for him and everyone really), he had a very public and scandalous moral failure. Of course, his ministry had ended in disgrace, but recently, after years away from the pulpit, he had begun to preach at a small country church. So there he was, desiring to be in the fellowship of preachers he would have mentored in days gone by. Providentially, the retreat leader started the meeting of these dozen or so with a practice that mimicked most Alcoholics Anonymous meetings. Instead of the usual introductions, he encouraged these men of God to introduce themselves with the line, "Hello, my name is _____, and I'm a sinner."

One by one, each man around the circle acknowledged his sin until it came to the older preacher mentioned above. He quietly, but firmly introduced himself in a way that changed the entire mood and spirit of the retreat. "Hello, my name is _____, and I'm an adulterer." He had taken the confession a step further. Everyone had admitted their sinful nature, but he had named his sin, the one that everyone in the room was aware of and from which he had repented. I'm blessed by that moment because I have learned in my own life, and that of others, repentance isn't real until you specifically name the sin you're repenting from.

That brings us to our verses for this day. Our challenge is not to generally pray, "Father…forgive us our debts, as we also forgive our debtors" (Matthew 6:12), but to call our sins by name as the apostle does in Ephesians 4. Let's practice. As an exercise in spiritual formation today, take a few minutes to consider each of the eight sins that are listed in these Scriptures. In each, I will provide a few brief examples of how each is often exhibited in our lives and a sentence to help articulate our repentance before the Father. WARNING: Reflexively, you will resist writing down particular sins in your life for fear that someone may read this book and find out (shocker) that you are a sinner. Please take the scary step. Get rid of it. Put it away. Repent.

Falsehood. This sin has to do with deceiving others into believing something that we know to be false. This can be as subtle as not telling someone the whole truth when they ask or denying you've done something you know you have done.

Everything from "tell them I'm not here," to lying on your résumé. Examine your life. Is there anything that is not true? "Father, my name is _____ and I have been false and I want to put it away."

Anger (wrath). This sin is an emotion that expresses itself when things don't go our way resulting in a verbal or physical outburst. Anger can come from parents who are frustrated by a child's action or in the midst of an argument with your spouse. Sporting events seem to be a place where competitive nature brings anger to athletes and fans alike. When were you last angry? Deal with it. "Father, my name is _____ and I have been angry; I want to put it away."

Stealing. Anytime we take something that is not ours without asking to borrow it, we have stolen: money from mom's purse; personal copies at work; intentionally loafing when you are being paid to work; not giving back to Jesus' church; downloading movies or music illegally. Anyone? "Father, my name is _____ and I have stolen and I want to put it away."

Corrupting talk. The word corrupt in this passage refers to something that is rotten and used most often in connection to fruits. Corrupt talk rots conversation and those around you, i.e., common curse words; words that profane the name of God, Christ, or the Holy Spirit; words that are filled with hate and insults. Often this sin accompanies anger. Analyze your words for a minute. "Father, my name is _____ and my speech is corrupt and I want to put it away."

Bitterness. Bitter is one of four tastes in the human experience and this word is representative of a soul that dwells on the negative past and unpleasant disappointments of life. With this sin, bitterness becomes a state of mind in which one views all of life and people in a negative way because things have not gone one's way. Are you bitter today? "Father, my name is _____ and I have been bitter and I want to put it away."

Clamor. Probably a sin you've never considered before is this word which means to cry out as you might at a funeral in mourning. But since mourning isn't a sin, it seems that the apostle is talking about crying out in a loud and boisterous way that is either insincere or bringing attention to oneself. Is your volume and demonstration an attention getting device for you? "Father, my name is _____ and have clamored, and I want to put it away."

Slander. The sin of slander is to say something about another that isn't true and with intention to hurt them and their reputation. Interestingly, the word used here is where we get our word "blasphemy" and it is used mostly in relation to God's name (i.e. saying something that is not true about God). Social media has become an easy place to exhibit slander. Have you damaged another's name? "Father, my name is _____ and I have slandered someone and I want to put it away."

Malice. Finally, we come to a word that is related to a couple of the sins above, but specifically is a desire for someone else's ill will. Malice is revenge. Malice is rejoicing at your enemy's disaster. Malice is sabotaging another's world to bring pain. Is there someone you'd really like to see fail (or worse)? Put it away. "Father, my name is _____ and I have malice in my heart that I want to put away."

DAY 20 - RECEIVE THE WORD

James 1:21

"Therefore put away all filthiness and rampant wickedness and receive with meekness the implanted word, which is able to save your souls."

Regardless of your gardening expertise, you can grow anything if the soil is receptive and good seed is planted. A few years ago, my wife asked me to get rid of the fall pumpkins that had decorated our porch and home. So I did what any good husband would do. I threw them in a corner of our back yard against a fence. Yes, I purposely threw them against the fence to experience the explosion (it's a guy thing). Anyway, you may have guessed what happened. That next spring, we began to notice vines sprouting in the corner of our back yard, and soon little orange blossoms appeared, and shortly after that, full-grown pumpkins. I had unintentionally grown a pumpkin patch.

Believe it or not, my accidental "green thumb" and today's reading go hand in hand. Pumpkins grew in my backyard because a seed was implanted in unexpectedly good soil. Likewise, we grow as the word of God is implanted in the good soil of our souls that is constantly "putting away" sin. That's James' formula for growing. As we repent of sin, the soil of our souls is more and more receptive to the word of God and growth happens. Today let's consider these two essential conditions for spiritual growth in our Christ following life.

Let's begin by identifying "the word" being implanted. The Greek term translated "word" in our verse today is the word "logos." This obviously points to the Living Word, Jesus. This is how John described Jesus in John 1:1, "In the beginning was the word (logos) and the word (logos) was with God and the word (logos) was God." Jesus is the spoken word of God come to life, and he alone is the seed of God planted in our hearts to grow our faith. However, the prophets, the early church, and even Jesus himself understood the written Scriptures to be about him, and therefore seed implanted in us. This is why the Bible is also rightly referred to as the word of God. Which does James intend here? Both.

We know that the seed of the word of God is good seed, but as Jesus explains in his parable about the sower and the seed (see Matthew 13), the condition of the soil is also necessary for growth. According to James, the seed and soil work together when we "put away" sin (here filthiness and wickedness), and "receive with meekness the implanted word" of God. This is where our theme of repentance comes in. The word for "receive" in this verse has the idea of being willingly and readily receptive. Along with this, "meekness" represents a humility of soul. In other words, our hearts become good soil as we humbly and willingly expose ourselves to the word of God.

To see how "putting away" and "receiving the word" work together for our repentance, let's consider these three powerful scriptures about the word that is the necessary seed for growth.

Receive the word as the way. The word of God is designed to show us the right way. In Psalm 119 (a very long song dedicated to the psalmist's love for the word of God), we find the words "Your word is a lamp to my feet and a light to my path" (Psalm 119:105). To follow Jesus is to acknowledge that he is the only way, the one path, the narrow road to God. But we also receive the Bible in such

83

a way. When we read the word of God (as we have throughout this book), we must receive it as being right. Many times, the soil of our souls and those who call themselves Christians are not receptive to the word because we have not made it the standard. More and more we live in a culture that insists on defining "right" as something that sounds good, feels good, and does good. But much of what is called right in our world is heading the wrong way. We must "put away" this worldly teaching and receive the Bible as a guide for our feet and light for our path.

Receive the living word. We don't receive the word as some ancient, outdated writings that are somehow out of touch with current reality. What makes our scriptures always relevant is that they are always alive. If the spoken word of God is eternally alive, and if we follow the living word of God (Jesus), then we must accept that the written word is living as well. That's what Hebrews says about the scriptures, "For the word of God is living and active…" (Hebrews 4:12a). This means that every time we read the Bible, it meets us where we are. It speaks into our life situation each and every time. This is why people often say, "I've never noticed that before" when reading the word. Personally, I have read, studied, and memorized the Bible for decades and yet, the words are always fresh, new, and applicable to my life. The word is about here and now because it is alive.

Receive the word deeply. When we spend time in the word, we also notice how it gets deep into our soul. Hebrews 4:12 continues by telling us that this "word of God… is sharper than any two edged sword, piercing to the division of soul and of spirit, of joints and marrow, and discerning the thoughts and intentions of the heart" (Hebrews 4:12b). The word of God, like a Roman sword cutting through an opponent, gets past the outer layer of our lives and touches us in the deepest parts of our soul. The reason that reading the word of God is so important is that it cuts past our self-lies, the attitudes we have grown accustomed to, and the sinful actions that have become habits. When we receive the word, we allow God's ways to reveal to us the sins that are deep and sometimes hidden.

Receive the word to grow. Finally, the implanted word is useful for helping me repent and get past my sin so that I can be equipped to do what God has called me to do. II Timothy 3:16 says, "All Scripture is breathed out by God and profitable for teaching, for reproof, for correction, and for training in righteousness. That the man of God may be complete, equipped for every good work." Time does not permit us to completely expose this verse, but the metaphors of a student learning in school and an athlete training for competition, explain what the word of God implanted in us does.

It's obvious isn't it? If we want to grow, we must be people of the book. Time in God's word both defines the sins we must put away, and plants his DNA deeply in our hearts. This is the salvation James is speaking to us today.

DAY 21 - AT THE FIRST

Revelation 2:4&5

---

*"But I have this against you, that you have abandoned the love you
had at the first. Remember therefore from where you have fallen;
repent, and do the works you did at the first. If not, I will come
and remove your lamp stand from its place, unless you repent."*

"At the first," driving a brand new car is one of life's great
experiences. I'm not talking about a car that's new to you,
perhaps one that your parents gave you when you turned 16 and
got your license, or one that a generous friend sold or gave to
you. I'm talking about a brand new, no-previous-owner, drive-
off-the-dealer's-lot car. It is not something I experienced until
well into adulthood and several years into marriage, but when
I did, it was awesome. What's so great about getting a new car?
Well, everything.

A new car looks good. The exterior color is a freshly painted,
brilliant, shiny, and an unscratched version of itself. The tires still
have plenty of tread and black polish. The seats are not stained
and the dashboard is not dusty. A new car works. The brakes don't
squeal. All of the controls light up and every switch works. The
controls to the sound system and every speaker give you great
sound. Taillights, brake lights, headlights and interior lights all

light up. Turn signals blink and windshield wipers wipe. A new car also smells good. Somehow, fresh leather, clean floor carpets, newly stitched cloth, plastic and chrome come together for an intoxicating smell. It's such a good smell that you can actually purchase a "new car smell" air freshener.

Now, if you're reading this chapter and you've never experienced a "new car," don't worry. The truth is the "new" wears off pretty fast. Usually within weeks of owning a new car, someone has scratched or dented it in a parking lot. Three or four months more into the new car experience a door light is not working, the floorboard carpet is stained from shoe residue, and the paint is barely visible beneath a layer of dirt. Give it a year, and the inside smells like spilled coffee, stale french fries, and the family dog. And just like that, the car that you loved so much "at the first" isn't so special anymore. It is simply a way to get from here to there.

This new car reality gets us close to our verses for the day and our final scripture about repentance. I know, I know, comparing a new car to Jesus is an illustration that breaks down pretty quickly. However, the point is still made. The love that seems so fresh, new, and exciting at the beginning of our walk with Christ has a tendency to fade. This appears to be the situation with our first century brothers and sisters who made up the church in the Roman metropolis of Ephesus. As noted in our verses above, Jesus has only one, but very important thing against this congregation. They have abandoned the love they had at the first and Jesus warns them to repent.

It's not that this wasn't a great church. By looking at the entire letter to the church at Ephesus, we find that Jesus has a lot of good to say to them (Revelation 2:1-7). Not surprisingly, they have a solid faith and sound theology. This is probably due to what we know about this congregation historically and biblically. The church had learned the Christian faith from some of the most gifted teachers. Early on, a great revival was sparked when the apostle Paul taught for two years in their city (see Acts 19:9-20). Besides this, the leadership of the young pastor Timothy, preaching of Apollos, and mentoring of Priscilla and Aquila, built upon the strong foundation of faith that had taken root. Finally, they seem to have been the home church of the apostle John three generations after it began.

But theology wasn't their only strength. Jesus says that he is aware of their works and their toil for his name. He also recognizes their patience. I imagine that if you attended First Church of Ephesus circa 95 A.D. you would be impressed with their solid preaching, their service to the community, and their patient interaction with the pagan world around them. It was a great church. But something was missing and that something was the love they had at the first.

Twice in these verses, Jesus calls them to repent. Not from some worldly sin, but from their spiritual apathy. This is a common struggle for us Christ followers. As we mature, it's possible for our faith to become a routine of discipline, knowledge and service, and miss the point of Jesus altogether. Jesus desires relationship. Remember? God so loved the world (relationship according to John 3:16). The father has loved us with a great love (relationship according to Ephesians 2:4). We love him because he first loved us (relationship according to I John 4:19). He has called us friends (relationship according to John 15:12-15). Relationship with Jesus is not all emotional, but it does include emotion. And that emotion is love.

Do you love Jesus? That's the repentance question for today. If the answer is not "yes," then repentance (remember the word means "to change your mind") is what Jesus is calling you to. Jesus' threat to "come and remove your lamp stand from its place, unless you repent" should be taken seriously. Not because you are afraid that Jesus is going to come and literally take you out of his church, but that the flame of your love is extinguished and no longer an influence in the world around you. If our love for Christ doesn't shine, there's no need for it to be on a lamp stand.

Before heading into our all-church dedication experience, let's rekindle our love for Jesus. Maybe you'll want to listen to a favorite worship song, read a Bible verse that stirs you, or spend some time listing the things you personally love about him on the "your story" page. Along the way, pray for the Spirit to move you back to that first love, back to the time when you first decided to follow him with all of your heart. Go back to the way it was at the first.

DAY 22 - WITNESS

Joshua 24:26&2

"And Joshua wrote these words in the Book of the Law of God. And, he took a large stone and set it up there under the terebinth tree that was by the sanctuary of the Lord. And Joshua said to all the people, 'Behold, this stone shall be a witness against us, for it has heard all the words of the Lord that he spoke to us. Therefore is shall be a witness against you, lest you deal falsely with your God.'"

The kind and authoritative Judge peers over the massive desk known as "the bench" and remarks, "You have made a very compelling case friend; do you have any further witnesses?" The elder lawyer replies, "Yes your honor, I do happen to have one more witness, but this one is a bit unorthodox." "Believe me when I say 'I've seen it all before'", replied the robed and white haired man. "I know you have" the counselor Joshua chuckled, "and I realize you already know what this witness brings to the case, but this is my star witness. The following testimony will verify everything that has been said by me and the people on trial today." "Well then, proceed" the Judge gently ordered. "Your honor, I'd like to call 'the stone' to the witness stand." And with that, the trial for Israel's commitment to God ended.

This make believe courtroom scene may seem a bit farfetched,

90

but it is a literal interpretation of the figurative language Joshua is using to make his point to the people of Israel. Now that the people have articulated their choice to serve God, and have put away their idols and false gods; Joshua uses trial language these people would have understood to mark the importance of this occasion. Like a defense lawyer, he has made his case for God. Like a court stenographer, he has written down every word. And, like a prosecutor, he has pointed to a witness. The witness is a large stone that he had moved to rest underneath a certain Terebinth tree near their place of worship. From this time forward when the people of Israel saw this stone, its presence alone would recall this day, these words, and these promises of fidelity towards God. This was a momentous consecration for the people of God, and this rock would witness against anyone who broke the promises made on that day.

Typically, the word that Joshua uses here would be used to describe a real live human because giving testimony is something only a living being could do. This simple Hebrew word, "ada" meant to give a testimony, to tell what one has seen. According to the Law of Moses, someone could not be convicted, found guilty, or even brought to trial without two or three witnesses (Deuteronomy 19:15). However, on the occasion that one brought an accusation against another, the elders of the town were often called to the town gate to hear the testimony. One by one, each witness would come to give his or her side of the story, what they had seen, what they had heard, and what they knew about this case. The witness was a powerful and important component for determining the truth.

In the same way that our spiritual ancestors did almost 3,500 years ago, from time to time we are called to articulate our intentions about following Jesus and serving him in his church. Their simple statement of faith was "The Lord our God we will serve, and his voice we will obey" (v. 24). You might call it their vision statement. This confession summed up every action and priority for their entire life. Simply stated: "serve God, obey God."

Today, when we come to baptism, we also make a statement of faith (from the apostle Peter's "good confession" in Matthew 16): "I believe that Jesus is the Christ, the son of the living God and I take him as my Lord and Savior." In this testimony, we publicly declare that since Jesus is God he is the only one we can trust with our lives (Lord) and eternities (Savior).

For those of us who call Eastview home, we have articulated how we intend to live our Christian lives in our vision statement. By faith and prayer we are becoming "a fearless church of Christ followers, whose ridiculous love and dangerous witness are irresistible." It's a testimony easily worn on a t-shirt and not so easily lived out day by day. So let's consider the different pieces of this statement before we take the witness stand.

"A fearless church of Christ followers" implies three realities. First, it speaks to community. We are a church. A collection of imperfect people who have been saved, changed, and empowered by Jesus. Which leads to the second reality. Because he has done so much for us, we follow him. He is the way. His way is best. He has the answers. He knows what's coming. He has a plan for us. Third, and finally, if all of the above is true, we can be fearless. It's not that life isn't scary; it's just that Jesus is bigger than all our fears. Therefore, we fearlessly follow him.

"...whose ridiculous love" reveals how we respond to others in light of our following. The love of Christ for us is something that could be ridiculed (the word from which we get ridiculous). He loved us when we didn't love him. In fact, he laid down his life – dying on the cross for us while we were his sworn enemies (see Romans 5:10). Since we have received this love that can only be described as ridiculous, we can offer it to others. We are committed to loving those who are not like us. We are committed to loving those who are not easy to love. We are committed to loving those who can't love us back. We are committed to those who won't love us back. We are marked by our love for others.

"…and dangerous witness" describes how we share the good news of what Jesus has done for us and can do for others. The idea of dangerous witness comes from the Greek word "martureo" which is the counterpart to the Hebrew word we have looked at above. It means to testify or to witness. Early on, however, this word took on a different meaning as the first Christians were killed for their testimony about Jesus. This is where we get the word "martyr." We may never be killed for sharing our faith, but we do realize there is some risk involved in sharing Jesus with our family and friends. And, we are willing to witness anyway because the truth of Christ is worth dying for.

Back to Joshua 24. There we find that the stone wasn't the only witness on that day to everything that was said and heard. Millions of people, men and women, young and old, were witnesses of each other's testimony. In verse 22, "Joshua said to the people, 'you are witnesses against yourselves…'". In other words, they all heard each other commit themselves to the Lord anew. As you pray and read this week, let me encourage you to state or restate your commitment to God in the presence of a witness or witnesses. Make an opportunity to share with another Christ follower what you believe about Jesus and how you intend to follow him. It may be as simple as affirming the vision statement we have just reviewed, affirming the good confession from when first believed, or writing a confession about Jesus in your own words. Whatever the case, in preparation for the Joshua 24 all church experience, make sure you have prayerfully considered what you truly believe and how you intend to live it out.

DAY 23 - TWO OR THREE

Deuteronomy 19:15

"A single witness shall not suffice against a person for any crime or for any wrong in connection with any offense that he has committed. Only on the evidence of two witnesses or of three shall a charge be established."

For a golfer there is no greater or rarer achievement than a "hole-in-one," but if he is alone, it really doesn't matter. In those unfortunate driving incidents where two cars back into the same place at the same time, someone who saw the whole thing can help determine who was at fault. When a lawyer is putting together an argument for innocence, the testimony of his client's character can make or break the case. When two young siblings get into a fight over a toy dispute, another brother or sister may help mom and dad determine "who started it." In every one of these scenarios, a witness is necessary to validate the truth. An eyewitness can testify to a golfer's shot, a driver's innocence, a defendant's character, and which sibling is to blame. A witness helps get to the truth and what is fair.

This is why God has so much to say in his word about witness. He is a God of truth and justice and desires for his people to live in both. And so this rule from Deuteronomy becomes the perpetual standard for people of God when it comes to judging someone who has been accused of a crime or offense. According to the verse above, the law given by Moses states that one witness is not enough to convict. Only with the corroborating testimony of two or three witnesses would an accusation be considered in the ancient Jewish court of law.

Again, we are reminded that our Heavenly Father desires the truth. In fact, truth is so important to him, especially as it pertains to our relationships with each other, that he addresses it in the Ten Commandments. One of his ten rules for godly living is "You shall not bear false witness against your neighbor" (Exodus 20:16). We sometimes understand this as a prohibition against lying (and to be sure, God hates lying), but this law specifically addresses giving false testimony about someone, claiming they did or said something they never did or said. Though bearing false witness was prohibited, a law requiring two or three witnesses would protect God's people from being wrongly accused and convicted.

From this point on, all courtroom cases (most often the city gates where the elders assembled) in Israel would require this minimum number of witnesses. But what you may not know is that this standard of truth and justice migrated into the life of the church and still stands to this day. In the New Testament, this standard moves from defendants in a courtroom to relational interactions between brothers and sisters in the church. Specifically, this witness number standard of "two or three" is still useful in today's church in three ways:

Personal relations.

In Matthew 18, Jesus himself is teaching about conflicts in the church. Why do conflicts happen in the church? Because people are in the church. So Jesus teaches that when someone in the church sins against another, the offended brother or sister should go to that person one on one and seek reconciliation. Unfortunately, this practice is often skipped in lieu of gossip (telling others that someone has offended you) causing much pain in the body of

Christ. If someone has offended you, go tell him or her. Prayerfully, they will listen and unity will be restored. However, Jesus foresaw that this might not be enough in every situation. So, in Matthew 18:16 he recalls this Old Testament standard, "But if he does not listen, take one or two others along with you, that every charge may be established by the evidence of two or three witnesses." In other words, the reconciliation of two Christians may be reached through two or three witnesses.

Church relations.

Another instance where church witnesses became important is found in the troubled, first century church at Corinth. This church had lots of issues addressed in Paul's first letter to this pagan-converted congregation. Among other things, these Christians had serious divisions, tolerated sexual sin, were drunk during communion, and were taking one another to court! And though the apostle had addressed all these and more, this disagreeable church still had issues that threatened to divide them. So as he ends his second letter, he invokes this Old Testament standard, "This is the third time I am coming to you. Every charge must be established by the evidence of two or three witnesses" (II Corinthians 13:1). When it comes to resolving disagreements within the church, two or three Christians help establish and verify the truth.

Leader relations.

Finally, this standard of accusation is applied to those who lead in the church. You may recall that Paul is coaching Timothy (his son in the faith) as he pastors the congregation at Ephesus. Timothy is young and inexperienced in dealing with church administration. Maybe he is unsure about how he should handle complaints against leaders like he and the elders of the church. So Paul invokes our verse for the day. "Do not admit a charge against an elder except on the evidence of two or three witnesses" (I Timothy 5:19). Elders in the church are to be respected in such a way that only criticism that is verified by two or three is even considered. Leadership comes with much weight and responsibility and with it protection of false accusation.

Ironically, Jesus, who being one with God, established this law of truth and justice, and was denied it. During his mock trial on the night Jesus was betrayed "...the chief priests and the whole counsel were seeking false testimony against Jesus that they might put him to death, but they found none, though many false witnesses came forward" (Matthew 26:59-60a). In the end, Jesus didn't get justice and truth during his trial, but he secured justice and truth by his death, burial, and resurrection. Since we have been forgiven and cleansed of all falsehood, let us seek to be faithful witnesses who tell the truth and seek the truth in all things.

DAY 24 - IN WRITING

Deuteronomy 31:26

"Take this Book of the Law and put it by the side of the ark of the covenant of the Lord your God, that it may be there for a witness against you."

Okay, here's a confession. Throughout my life I have signed my name at the bottom of many documents that I have not previously read. I have signed multi-paged contracts for home mortgages, gym memberships, insurance policies, and car rentals. These days, a signature is not even needed; a simple click on "accept" to a long list of terms will gain me access for many online services, apps, rentals, and purchases. Again, there are pages of terms and conditions, but I don't think I have read a single line of any of them.

While you may think this practice of signing without reading is irresponsible, I know I am not alone. Most of us simply don't have the time to read five pages of disclaimers before using the gym's treadmill or sort through paragraphs of legalese on the back of a baseball ticket. Besides, most of the language is written in such a way that few people would understand even after reading. Still, someone has taken the time to put in writing all of the expectations, promises, obligations, and responsibilities inherent with a contract. And when I sign my name on the bottom line, I'm responsible for what is written regardless of my knowledge of what is in writing. The same is true when we sign up by faith to follow Jesus.

This gets us to our verse for the day. "This Book of the Law" is God's agreement with his people. Exactly what is this "Book of the Law?" At the least, it could be as narrow as the Ten Commandments and at the most, as broad as the Pentateuch (first five books of our Old Testament), or somewhere in between (all of the laws written therein). My studies have caused me to conclude "the Book of the Law" references the entirety of the books attributed to Moses (Genesis through Deuteronomy) and ultimately, the book we call the Bible. In any case, the words in this covenant book, like the documents mentioned above, include every promise, expectation, obligation, description, law, example and responsibility for relationship with God.

Unlike gods from Greek mythologies and other world religions, we don't have to guess what God is thinking or how he will react. He has plainly stated what we are signing up for when we follow him by faith and he has taken every measure to communicate it to us, whether we have paid attention or not. This is why Bible leaders like Joshua regularly read all of these words within the hearing of the ancient people of God. "And afterward he read all the words of the law, the blessing and the curse, according to all that is written in the Book of the Law" (Joshua 8:34). Today, pastors and teachers still work to communicate all that is written in the word of God so that people can know what God is all about. There are two important questions to Gods' contract with mankind that help us know what we are signing up for.

What has God said is wrong and what are the consequences?

Many people have an image of God that is not founded on how he describes himself in the Bible. In a sense, most have formed God into what they want him to be – a fun loving, lenient grandpa who always gives us candy, loves to watch us play, and winks at mischief. But this is not what he has put in writing about himself. The truth is he is very specific about all of the wrong actions committed by mankind and all of the punishment (and ultimately death) that comes from this sin. A simple search on any number of Bible websites will help give insight into such words as "sin," "transgressions," and "cursed." These verses and more God has put in writing to keep us from harm. He has written them down as a warning.

What has God said is right and what are the blessings?

Most of us are likely a bit more familiar with the blessings of God, but we are probably a little fuzzy on who exactly God blesses. We have a tendency to quote, "God works everything together for the good…" while ignoring who this promise is for (ie. "…those who love him and are called according to his purpose" (Romans 8:28, KJV). God is not ashamed to put in writing his desire to bless us, and the ways he intends to do so. Again, a simple search on a Bible website with words like "promise," "blessing," and "eternal life" will reveal God's intentions for our good. These verses and more God has put in writing to give us hope for a blessed future.

Of course, all these written words of cursing and blessing were fulfilled and revealed in the person of Jesus. He is God's living word communicated to us in the flesh. Through him God agrees to take away the curse of our sin by Jesus' death and give us eternal life through Jesus' resurrection. This contract is not lengthy or confusing. It is an agreement summed up in one word: Jesus. And anyone can sign on the dotted line by faith.

Back to our verse from Deuteronomy, Moses is saying that this book of the Law becomes a witness because in it God has warned us of the consequence of our sin and also shown us the way to eternal life in him. This is one contract we should never enter into without reading God's fine print. There will be no excuses later when we say, "we didn't know" or "that's not fair" because God has been upfront about everything. His book gives testimony. Through God's written word he has shown himself to be fair and through his living word, Jesus, he has revealed his great mercy, love, and grace. It would be tragic not to read and know all that he has put in writing.

Like many of you, I have had to live up to covenants I didn't read, but signed anyway. I've gotten rid of the family dog because of a home owners' association rule that I was not aware of. I've had to stay in a cell phone contract longer than I wanted as stipulated in the agreement. I've experienced the pain of paying for extra mileage on a rental car because I didn't read the limits on the contract. No excuses. I didn't read. I didn't know. Still I signed. It's my fault. In the same way, when it's all said and done, claims of God's injustice or lack of clarity will fall on deaf ears. After all, he has been very clear and has put it all in writing.

You may want to take a few minutes today to write some words of interest in "your story" notes. Beside each, put a verse or two and what you learned about the word in question.

DAY 25 - ETHAN'S SONG

Psalm 89:33-37

"but I will not remove from him my steadfast love or be false to my faithfulness. I will not violate my covenant or alter the word that went forth from my lips. Once for all I have sworn by my holiness; I will not lie to David. His offspring shall endure forever, his throne as long as the sun before me. Like the moon it shall be forever, a faithful witness in the skies."

You just read parts of an ancient song obviously written during a time when the Jewish nation and stability of the throne in Jerusalem seemed to be in question. We don't know the circumstances that inspired these words. It may have been inspired during the time of David's grandson Rehoboam, when the kingdom was divided between Israel and Judah. It may have entered the national songbook during any other number of catastrophes, wars, or natural disasters brought upon the Old Testament people of God through their unfaithfulness.

Whatever the circumstance, and obviously in the midst of national duress, Ethan the Ezrahite, wrote a song of God's faithfulness. And in this song, he introduces yet another strange courtroom scene in which God the judge becomes God the defendant, and the moon becomes a faithful witness. Led by the Spirit, Ethan creatively allows God take the stand on his behalf to testify and give witness of his character. The words "covenant" in verse 34 and "sworn" in verse 35 give indication that the the song about God's faithfulness takes place in a courtroom. In question is his relationship to David and his promise to establish his throne forever.

The promise.

In fact, God acknowledges making a promise to the famous king David. In II Samuel 7 God promises David that the kingdom would be passed on to his offspring, that this son would build a house for God's name, and that his throne would be established. All of this was fulfilled through David's son Solomon, who inherited the kingdom of his father, built the temple in Jerusalem, and whose fame, power, wealth, and wisdom was known throughout the world. This was only the beginning because the well-known promise that Ethan writes about comes to David in II Samuel 7:16, "And your house and your kingdom shall be made sure forever before me. Your throne shall be established forever."

It's easy to see why the people of Israel would despair when it seemed as if the throne and kingdom were slipping away. They had a vested interest in the promise. As long as there was a king on the throne of David, they would remain the people of God. But as Ethan writes, (again, the exact circumstance is unknown), it appears that the "eternal" throne of David is coming to an end. No more heirs from David's house. No more house of God. No more people of God. Will God keep his promise?

God is faithful.

So through this song of God's faithfulness, God takes the stand as his own character witness. "I will not be false to my faithfulness" he begins and then restates it in several ways. If I were to paraphrase these verses, God is saying, "I don't break contracts or back out of agreements. When I say something, I mean it. You'll never find me saying, 'I was just kidding.' I don't have to change even one word of what I have spoken because I mean every word I say." And then raising his right hand, "I swear by my holiness that I will not lie to David. I will keep my promise about his offspring enduring forever." The problem with the people of Israel is that they had been faithless to God. They had broken their promise to follow, serve, and obey God. The pain in their world is a result of their being unfaithful, but the unfaithfulness of God's people doesn't affect God's faithfulness. As the New Testament writer says concerning rebellious Israel, "What if some were unfaithful? Does their faithlessness nullify the faithfulness of God? By no means! Let God be true though every one were a liar" (Romans 3:3&4).

God's love remains.

The last part of God's defense answers a question often thought about by the people of God, even if they don't ask it aloud. "Has God stopped loving us?" Throughout the Old Testament, we find this truth about the love of God; it is steadfast. In fact, the word for steadfast love here is the Hebrew word "chesed" (pronounced "keh – sed" like you're clearing your throat on the "k"). This rich word, translated in the older Bible versions as "lovingkindness" is mercy, love, pity, favor, and faithfulness all rolled into one. It describes a love that chooses to love in an unconditional way. This love is not deserved but freely given, and by choice this love cannot be taken away. When God says, "I love you" it's because of his loving nature and it cannot be taken away.

In his defense, God says that his love for David will never end. "I will not remove from him my steadfast love (chesed)." For reasons we may never understand until we see God face to face, God loved David. And that love remained throughout David's adultery, lying, and murder associated with his relationship with Bathsheba. Solomon was also unfaithful as mentioned in that Scripture quoted earlier, "when he commits iniquity…my steadfast love will not depart from him…" (II Samuel 7:14&15). God just doesn't give up on those he loves. He doesn't break up. He doesn't divorce. He never quits on us – even when we deserve it.

Jesus proves it.

As Exhibit "A" God presents his son Jesus Christ. In Luke 1:32 and 33 the angel says to Mary in the traditional Christmas story, "He will be great and will be called the Son of the Most High. And the Lord God will give to him the throne of his father David, and he will reign over the house of Jacob forever, and of his kingdom there will be no end" (the one who sits on the forever throne of David). In other words, the eternal nature of David's throne is spiritually and eternally fulfilled through Jesus Christ. As the descendant of David, born in Bethlehem and named "king of the Jews" on the cross in Jerusalem, Jesus was the fulfillment of God's promise. Case dismissed. God is faithful. God can be trusted. God loves us. Spend some time thinking of God's faithfulness today.

DAY 26 - NEW COVENANT

Jeremiah 31:31-34

"Behold, the days are coming, declares the Lord, when I will make a new covenant with the house of Israel and the house of Judah... For this is the covenant that I will make with the house of Israel after those days, declares the Lord: I will put my law within them, and I will write it on their hearts. And I will be their God, and they shall be my people. And no longer shall each one teach his neighbor and teach his brother, saying, 'Know the Lord,' for they shall all know me, from the least of them to the greatest, declares the Lord. For I will forgive their iniquity, and I will remember their sin no more."

The world of professional sports leagues, athletes, cable networks, and team owners is dominated with contract talk. In our sports crazed world, we know that billions of dollars are spent each year to bring us the entertainment fans desire. But how do we know who gets paid what? In a word, "contracts." Contracts between team owners and players determine in writing how much the athlete is paid to perform on the field, pitch, court, or ice. Often, incentive bonuses to win are included to raise the level of performance. Again, it's all in black and white. If the athlete does "A", the team owner will pay him or her "B". But this is only the beginning.

The owner in turn is under contractual obligations to his or her respective league to conduct and manage the team in a way that is beneficial to the other owners involved. They are in agreement with each other to market their team in such a way that they all make and split a significant amount of money. A major stream of this lucrative business is television and cable rights to allow fans access to their favorite teams, which requires (you guessed it) more contracts between leagues and broadcast entities. Somewhere in all of this mix are lawyers contracted to get bigger contracts for both themselves and their clients. The only ones not under contract... the fans who pay hundreds of dollars a pop to help finance all of these contracts.

The deal with contracts is that they expire. All of the contract examples given include a date when the agreement is no longer binding. The length of these written obligations range from one to ten years, but eventually, the covenant to pay and perform is concluded. This is why sports news is filled with contract negotiations, contract disputes, contract holdouts, and contract signings and re-signings. Did you know that God's Old Testament covenant expired? By his eternal wisdom, grace, and intention, the old contract based on the Law concluded when he signed a new contract with us. In fact, as indicated in our reading today, even as the old covenant was in place between God and his people, God spoke of a future and better covenant that he would establish.

In case, you've forgotten (or didn't know), I'll remind you that the words "covenant" and "contract" are essentially the same thing. "God's old and new covenant" is Bible terminology for "God's old and new contract." So, when God says, "I will make a new covenant" that's "not like the covenant I made with their fathers," he is proposing a new contract between him and us. There are three differences in these old and new documents.

A covenant of the heart.

The old covenant is one based on obedience to the law. The contract was literally written first on tablets of stone and then (as we have said) in the Book of the Law. The contract obligations were clear, written in great detail. No mistaking what was expected. Obey the laws or the contract is broken. There are two problems with the old covenant. First, no one could keep all the rules and everyone eventually broke the contract. The second problem was that one could follow the rules externally while missing the heart change God desired. So the new contract began with Jesus forgiving our hearts and continues by making us new day by day. The new contract is not about keeping laws, but rather a change of heart that "loves because he first loved us."

A covenant all will understand.

The second change in this covenant would be how all could understand it "from the least of them to the greatest." The first contract required a hierarchy of priests, rabbis, scribes, and tribal leaders. This was needed to help the people understand, comply with, and remember the hundreds of laws in the complex contract of Moses. But this new agreement summed up the entire law and prophets in one word: Jesus. No need for explanations of sacrifices and rituals needed. Now everyone in the kingdom is a priest and all that needs to be understood is that Jesus is Lord. Besides all of this, God's Holy Spirit lives in every believer to explain, guide, comfort, convict, correct, gift and empower. The very presence of God dwells in those who call Jesus Lord to give understanding of who he is and all he desires for us.

A covenant of forgiveness.

Finally, the new covenant was one of forgiveness instead of condemnation. The old covenant was a list of sins that constantly reminded us of just how sinful mankind truly is. As Paul says, "If it had not been for the law I would not have known sin" (Romans 7:7). To say it another way, the more we reviewed the contract, the more we realized we weren't living up to it. Thankfully, God wrote a new contract that allows us to stand before him sinless. He has commuted our sins because of his great mercy, which means we are no longer guilty. No matter what laws you have broken, promises you haven't kept, and rules you have ignored under the old contract, God offers us a new one. You may be thinking, "When can I change contracts?"

Well, the old covenant ended when Jesus drew up a new one by his death, burial, and resurrection. He rightly represented God in establishing this new agreement because though he was human, he was God in the flesh. So on the night in which he was betrayed, he very specifically proposes a new, fifteen-word contract: "This cup that is poured out for you is the new covenant in my blood" (Luke 22:20, see also Matthew 26:28 and Mark 14:24). The writer of Hebrews refers to Jesus as "the mediator of a new covenant" (Hebrews 12:24). This contract has no fine print. It doesn't need a lawyer to explain it. It requires nothing of us except faith; an admission that we are wrong and have trust in Jesus to save us and lead us. This covenant is not black ink on white paper, but red blood that pours from his hands, his sides, his face. And it covers us.

DAY 27 - GOOD FIGHT

I Timothy 6:12

"Fight the good fight of faith. Take hold of the eternal life to which you were called and about which you made the good confession in the presence of many witnesses."

I cannot prove that the apostle Paul was a sports fan, but I believe there is biblical evidence that he was. At the very least, he was greatly aware of the Roman culture in which he lived and their passion for sports and sporting entertainment. Of course, this would include one of the most ancient events, boxing. Through historic carvings, paintings, and writings, organized boxing can be dated back to at least 1,500 B.C. Perhaps the only professional sport to predate boxing is wrestling, and in his writings the apostle uses both as analogies for the Christian faith.

But here, as Paul considered a way to encourage his young son in the faith who was pastoring the church in Ephesus, he used fighting as a metaphor for the Christian walk. This is because Paul, like the master teacher Jesus, knew that sometimes a picture helps us understand deep and unexplainable concepts of faith. And the picture that comes to the apostle's mind in this early stage of Christianity, a picture that he knew Timothy would clearly understand, was that of boxing. I believe there are three lessons he intended for Timothy to grasp, and by the Holy Spirit's inspiration, us as well.

The good fight is painful.

Ancient boxing rules were simply brutal. As the sport grew, boxers wore leather straps across their knuckles, but that's about all as they usually boxed in the nude. The rules were simple: no eye gouging, no punches to the genitals, and no biting. The match ended when one of the boxers was incapacitated (knocked out or worse). If this took too much time, the official could speed the outcome by demanding both boxers stand face to face and trade punches until the match ended. The Greek word Paul uses in verse 12 will give us some insight to the enormity of the struggle. The word is "agonidzomai", which pronounced correctly, begins with our word "agony". Fighting in the first century was painful and sometimes deadly.

So what was Paul saying about the Christian faith? I believe he was communicating to Timothy that this life of testifying that Jesus is both Lord and Savior can be painful. Paul had experienced the pain of testimony, having been beaten, imprisoned, ridiculed, stoned, and left for dead. In the same way, his spiritual apprentice Timothy had been mocked, looked down on for his youth, debated, and ignored as he tried to lead the Ephesian congregation. So, faith is like a fight because it sometimes brings painful opposition.

This is still true 2,000 years later. Thousands of Christians worldwide are murdered, imprisoned, ridiculed, or shut out economically every day because of their faith. Even in our American culture, confessing faith in Christ can be painful. Aligning ourselves with the church and her true teachings can cause us to be ostracized from friends, co-workers, or family members. Some have resigned or been fired from lucrative professions for boldly displaying their faith. Many of us have lost friends or opportunities for advancement, and have been made fun of for our "outdated beliefs". We endure all of this, plus the pain of failures, tragedies, illnesses, and death that comes with the human experience.

The good fight doesn't back down.

All this talk of pain may cause us to want to shrink back and not be in the fight, but good faith, like a good fighter keeps going. He reminds Timothy to keep going back to that "good confession" that he made in the presence of many witnesses. Timothy knew it to be true then and Paul is encouraging him to "keep throwing punches" based on the validity of his testimony about Jesus now. In fact, in the following verse Paul notes that Jesus didn't back down either. Though he was hours from his imminent crucifixion, "… Christ Jesus…in his testimony before Pontius Pilate made the good confession" (I Timothy 6:13b). In this way, Jesus didn't back down from his fight against sin and death even though he knew the pain that lay ahead.

In the same way, we are called to stay in the fight. This is not to pretend that there are real challenges to our faith. Christians get tired. Christ followers get discouraged. People of faith have times of doubt, exhaustion, weakness, brokenness, depression, and fear. But we can stay in the fight because of God's Holy Spirit living inside of us. Our strength to daily confess our trust in Jesus, in spite of pain, is not a call to try harder or get stronger. Instead, it points to a strength that comes from God within. As Paul says in another place, "I can do all things through him who strengthens me" (Philippians 4:13). We only have to keep fighting.

The good fight of faith looks forward to the victory.

Finally, the good fight points victory. Of course, there were in ancient times like there are today, superior athletes who were undefeated. Though many challengers would come and go, fight after fight, the champion's victory was nearly guaranteed. This means that as the fight began, the favored boxer could fight with a confidence that victory would be his. He may endure some hard punches, incur some nasty injuries, and be pushed to the physical limit, but in the end, he would taste victory.

In the same way, our faith is guaranteed through Jesus Christ and his victory on the cross. Because he died, we are victorious over sin, and because he rose from the dead, we are victorious over death. No matter how impossible the victory seems, we know that we win through Jesus' death, burial, and resurrection. I believe this is why Paul reminds Timothy to "take hold of the eternal life to which you were called." Our daily focus on the eternal life promised in Christ changes the way I fight the good fight. I'm not worried about my future. I'm confident in Jesus. I'm done with earthly things and investing in eternal things. I have peace, joy, and am truly loved.

Spend some time today considering the fight and witness of your faith. Write your story in the space provided. Consider again "the good confession" – do you believe that Jesus is the Christ, the son of the Living God? In what ways does your life give witness to this truth before you even speak? Who knows that you are a Christ follower because you have told them? Think of some ways in which you could increase your dangerous witness – make your faith a little more visible and noticeable. Write it. Pray it. Do it. Fight the good fight.

DAY 28 - RUN

Hebrews 12:1&2

"Therefore, since we are surrounded by so great a cloud of witnesses, let us also lay aside every weight, and sin which clings so closely, and let us run with endurance the race that is set before us, looking to Jesus, the founder and perfecter of our faith, who for the joy that was set before him endured the cross, despising it's shame, and is seated at the right hand of the throne of God."

There is nothing quite like the roar of the crowd in an arena, coliseum, or stadium. Sometimes, as in the college stadiums at Michigan, Tennessee, and USC, there are over 100,000 spectators at full throat screaming, yelling, and cheering for teams and athletes in the midst of competition. Most often, this explosion of decibels and sound takes place when a great play is made – a touchdown in football, a goal in soccer, or a dunk in basketball. These feats and more demonstrate the adulation of the spectators for the greatness of their favorite sports stars, but there is another effect. There are times in the course of any athletic competition when the boisterous noise of the fans in the stands encourages the player in the stadium to soar to even greater heights of greatness.

This is what the writer of Hebrews is getting at in our verse for today. It's yet another sports metaphor from the Bible to help us understand our Jesus following life – the picture of a stadium full of witnesses. Again, the ancients were crazy about their sports with stadiums in every major city for horse races, gladiator games, and, of course, Olympic style competition. Specifically here, the Bible pictures a large arena full of spectators (i.e., "surrounded by so great a cloud of witnesses") rising to their feet as the runners near the finish line. The roar of thousands gives testimony to the greatness of these elite athletes and spurs them to run faster than ever before.

In the physical sense, we know who the spectators are. Fans from Ancient Greece from circa 300 B.C filled the stadium in Athens (the location of which can still be identified), to be entertained by runners, wrestlers, javelin throwers, etc... Fans in Rome filled the Coliseum to witness the physical feats of their favored gladiators in the first century (the same time this Bible verse was written). And fans in the United States fill gymnasiums and stadiums on high school and college campuses, as well as professional venues, in most mid-size and larger cities. There are literally, millions of fans every day who, through their loud cheers (testimony or witness), give encouragement to those in the race.

In the spiritual sense, the spectators are the great men and women of faith who have gone before us. We know this because Chapter 11 of the book of Hebrews is basically a "who's who" of faith from the Old Testament heroes. It includes the names we know like Abraham, Isaac, Jacob, David, and Moses, along with some lesser-known ones like Rahab, Barack, and Jephthah. Each of these and more are recognized for one thing. They had faith. This is why Hebrews 11 is often referred to as the "Faith Hall of Fame." Each person there, had lived and died in a way that declared faith in God and what he had promised. They were witnesses to God's greatness and provision. These and other people of faith are the spectators that now surround us according to Hebrews 12:1.

Imagine an Olympic stadium filled with toga and sandal wearing characters from the Bible, each with their Coke and popcorn in hand, watching the action on the field. Along with them, I don't think it's too much of a biblical stretch to add other people of faith who have gone before us. Maybe you'll picture your godly parents or grandparents who are no longer living. Perhaps, you can imagine a preacher from your youth, the person who first shared Jesus with you, or a spiritual mentor or friend who has passed away. Of course, the stands are filled with millions of others, whom you don't know, but are part of God's great family of faith that spans the centuries and the globe. These are other people, like yourselves, who through the ages have given their resources, their service, their words, and even their lives as a result of their testimony about Jesus. Imagine every person of faith who has ever lived watching us – the people of faith in the arena of humanity. Here are three thoughts on the witness of our lived-out faith.

In the arena.

We are in the arena. We are the competitors. We are not trying to win because that has already been assured in Christ. But, our faith matters. The testimonies we give at school, at work, at home, at the gym, in line and online are part of God's kingdom being played out in earth time. The thing to remember is that unlike basketball games, soccer matches, and track meets, the way we live out our witness is a matter of life and death. While it's true, many sporting events in the first century were athletic competitions; many were life and death fights between gladiators and Christians being devoured by lions. The truth is, each of our stories being played out in the arena of our lives is being observed by those who have gone before us. May we display the faith they did when they were in the game.

Run the race.

We are not just in the arena; we are running. Running is yet another powerful metaphor for the Christian life. And that is emphasized here. There are two important faith-running tips given here. 1) Get rid of extra weight, it will slow you down. Sin is the extra weight of the Christian life that keeps us from having the witness we could have without it. Often, we make our race harder by carrying the weight of those sins that we haven't let go of. The challenge is to let go to run better. 2) Run with endurance. Anyone who has ever run has faced moments of exhaustion when quitting seemed so attractive. The race of faith is not different. Not every day in the Christian life feels like victory, but the encouragement here is to keep running when the race seems the hardest because there is victory at the end.

Jesus as champion.

How can I know there is victory? Because the champion over sin and death has won. Jesus kept running as he faced his harshest trials. He endured because he focused on the joy at the end of the race. He would be victorious and sit in the chair of honor at the right hand of God. So, today, consider the arena of your race. Consider the spiritual spectators surrounding and cheering you on. Consider the ONE who is waiting for you at the finish line. Consider your victory in him. And run.

DAY 29 - LEGACY

Joshua 24:29-31

"After these things Joshua the son of Nun, the servant of the Lord, died, being 110 years old. And, they buried him in his own inheritance at Timnath-serah, which is in the hill country of Ephraim, north of the mountain of Gaash. Israel served the Lord all the days of Joshua, and all the days of the elders who outlived Joshua and had known all the work the Lord did for Israel."

Judges 2:10

"And there arose another generation after them who did not know the Lord or the work that he had done for Israel."

A year ago, my wife Sara and I were leading our church group on the final day of a spiritual pilgrimage through the Bible land of Israel in the city of Jerusalem. Next on the itinerary was a visit to the exposed part of Herod's first century construction on the Temple Mount known as "the Western Wall" or "the Wailing Wall." As we approached the security, our Jewish guide gave instructions for passing through the scanners, casually mentioning that Chrissy (one of the young ladies on our trip) should use an alternate entrance since she was pregnant. Suddenly our son and daughter-in-law, Mikey and Monica, ran to us and said, "We have something to tell you." They had just found out the night before that they were pregnant and were going to wait to tell us over dinner; but now they had to reveal their good news. Sara and I were going to be grandparents. We hugged. We cried. We laughed at the less-than-sacred situation as we rushed through security with hundreds of others.

All through the day, as the fact that my oldest son was going to have a kid came to mind, I teared up. These were tears of joy as I reflected on the reality that there would be yet another generation of the Baker family. Strangely, I thought of my grandpa and my dad who are no longer with us and I was struck with the immensity of family heritage and their legacy. As we settled into dinner later that evening, I asked Mikey if they had thought of any names for a boy. He gave me a "duh-are-you-serious?" look that I even had to ask. He said, "Dad, Michael Robert Baker III." If this child is a boy, he will be named after his father and grandfather. A legacy name that could easily span 100 years or more.

Names are not the only things passed on from generation to generation. Legacies come in all shapes and sizes, both good and bad. There are legacies of great marriages and broken homes. There are legacies of drug and alcohol abuse and legacies of faith. Some families pass weight issues from generation to generation, while others pass down Christmas traditions, recipes, and family occupations. This is not to mention the passing on of physical features: facial expressions, vocabulary, biases, prejudices, politics, and family history. All of these and more can be considered legacies that older generations leave long after they are gone.

A legacy is originally defined as money or possessions left behind through a will or bequest of one who has died, but the definition of legacy can be expanded as anything handed down from the past to those still living. This means that legacies are most often material (like the family farm), but they can also be attitudinal, philosophical, and more to our point for this study, spiritual.

As we come to the end of the Joshua 24 experience, we come to the death of Joshua. Remember, the book of Joshua began with the death of Moses and the passing of leadership on to Joshua. The question for us to consider now is whether these two powerful and accomplished leaders left a legacy. By all indications, the answer according to the description of Joshua at his death is a resounding "yes." Here's the line – "Joshua, the son of Nun, the servant of the Lord."

This description is identical to the one used for Moses beginning in Joshua 1:1: "…Moses, the servant of the Lord…" This line becomes the one description the author uses of Moses over 16 times throughout the book of Joshua. Not Moses, the lawgiver. Not Moses, the plague guy. Not Moses of the miracle staff. Not Moses, former prince of Egypt. The legacy of Moses was that he was called the servant of the Lord. What's significant about this is that Joshua didn't start off that way. He was "Joshua, Moses' assistant." This word indicates that Joshua served him by helping him accomplish his leadership responsibilities. But, what's impressive is that Joshua caught the legacy of Moses because at the end of his life, they were described in the same way – "servant of the Lord."

As parents, leaders, teachers, bosses, coaches, co-workers, fellow students, friends and neighbors, those around us may not catch what we say, but they will definitely catch how we live. When we leave this life and this world behind, what will our legacy be? What will be the one line description of our life that carries on to the next generation? It is an important consideration for our families and for our church families. Most of us will leave some family heritage associated with our name, some of us will leave a monetary inheritance, but all of us will leave a spiritual legacy of faith – good or bad.

You see, as we consider the possibilities of the legacies of faith that each of us may leave for our families and church; we must also acknowledge that there is another kind of legacy. If we don't keep our focus on the importance of passing on our spiritual experience, an entire generation may be lost. It is possible that a godly nation, a thriving church, and a Christian family could lose its way within one generation. Unfortunately this is the story of the people of Israel as noted in Judges 2:10 "…And there arose another generation after them who did not know the Lord or the work that he had done for Israel."

On the page provided below, reflect on what you think your current legacy is. What would your kids, spouse, work associates, etc… use to sum up who you are? Next to that, write what you would like your legacy to be. More than anything else, what impression do you want to pass on to future generations? Spend some time praying about this and commit to becoming the legacy you desire. Once more, refer to the appropriate study guide in the back of this book for additional spiritual exercises during this week of remembering.

DAY 30 - HEAR

Deuteronomy 6:4-6

"Hear, O Israel: The Lord our God, the Lord is one. You shall love the Lord your God with all your heart and with all your soul and with all your might. And these words that I command you today shall be on your heart. You shall teach them diligently to your children, and shall talk of them when you sit in your house, and when you walk by the way, and when you lie down, and when you rise. You shall bind them as a sign on your hand, and they shall be as frontlets between your eyes. You shall write them on the doorposts of your house and on your gates."

A trip to the Holy Land is an unparalleled life experience for someone who professes faith in Jesus. Like other countries one may visit, modern day Israel certainly has its touristy advantages. It boasts spectacular beaches, unique cuisine, beautifully rugged mountains, and cultural opportunities. But for people of the Christian faith, visiting the land of the Bible simply brings the black-on-white words of the Scripture to life.

Even the modern hotels in the secularized city of Tel Aviv demonstrate and highlight the daily living realities of things read in the nooks and crannies of the Bible. For example, if you stay in a hotel on a Saturday, you will experience a Sabbath elevator that stops at every floor. This is the preventative measure against the work of pressing a button, which would violate the sacred day of rest. Another oddity one may recognize comes from a law in Exodus 23:19 "you shall not boil a young goat in its mother's milk". Jewish rabbis have interpreted this as a mandate to separate meat from dairy products. This means your menu will be cheese but no meat at breakfast and meat but no cheese at dinner. No exceptions. Don't think about asking. No meat and cheese omelet for breakfast and no milk for dinner. Not to mention the unclean food called "bacon" is completely unavailable!

Today's verses that encourage parents to teach their children can also be experienced 3,500 years later in the everyday life of Jewish culture. In the airport, one will likely notice several orthodox Jewish men with leather straps around their arms and similar straps securing a little black box to their foreheads. Likewise, you may notice a small rectangular box adorning just about every door one enters (yes, every room of every hotel.) Both of these are literal interpretations of the words above "you shall bind them as a sign on your hand and they shall be as frontlets between your eyes. You shall write them on the doorposts…" Jewish people literally have little scrolls of these verses in boxes on their foreheads and on their doors entering their homes.

What's the point? Well, while I'm not sure God intended for parents to wear boxes on their heads and have miniature Bible verses on the doors of their houses, I'm quite sure of his intentionality when it comes to their role in spiritual legacy of their children. For God, the most important legacy is the faith parents pass on to their children. The number one job of a parent is to make sure their boy or girl knows the Lord and that they love him with all their heart, soul, and might. God knows that if the parent has bound (spiritually more than literally) the word of God on their heart and mind (forehead) and marked their houses with that same word, then the legacy of that family will be about faith in God.

Without doubt, parenting is one of the great challenges of life. A parent has to decide on whether to educate through home, public, or private schooling. A parent has to decide methods of discipline and rules at each stage of life. Parents set limits and expectations. Parents teach their children how to walk and talk, how to tie their shoes and brush their teeth, how to read and write, how to drive, and a million other things. And all this, with no prior experience. Surprisingly, parenting is not learned from a book and no one is naturally great at it. No, parenting is mostly generational. Parents parent as a result of how they were parented. When we raise children, some reject the parenting styles of our parents and do the opposite while others adopt their parents' methods and imitate them as best they can. Actually, parenting is usually combination of both.

Regardless of method, the result is that children in a family are very directly affected by the men and women who make up their respective family trees. And since this is true, there is nothing (and I repeat nothing), more important for a parent to dedicate themselves to, than continuing or establishing a strong faith in the children God has entrusted to them. Unfortunately, this generation of parents tends to wear themselves out allowing kids to be over involved, giving them more than they had, and trying to gain their friendship instead of their respect. But these things are unimportant in the grand scheme of things. According to Deuteronomy, there are two things that matter when it comes to really setting the priorities of the children in our families.

The first priority is talking to your children about your faith. Are you verbally expressing your faith in Jesus systematically and regularly to your children? Even great people of faith may assume their kids somehow understand, but I have found there is no substitute for speaking about your faith. This is what Moses is encouraging when he says, "talk of them when you sit in your house, and when you walk by the way, and when you lie down, and when you rise." To pass on our faith we must pray with our kids, read the Bible with our kids, and tell our kids what we believe about Jesus. This may include sharing our story of how we came to faith.

Along with this is the way we live the faith that we proclaim. Are you living your faith as sincerely as possible? The bottom line is that our children will by and large turn out to be like us. The question is, are we living a life that we will be happy with when we see it in the lives of our kids? If we want our kids to be generous, we will have to be generous. If we want our kids to go to church, we will have to go to church. If we want our kids to love Jesus, we will need to sincerely love Jesus. A parent's servanthood will translate into children serving and parent love for others will develop a love for all in the hearts of our kids. There is simply no substitute for living out the faith to help form the faith of future generations.

Take some time to think of your story and how your parents influenced you in word and deed. You may write down life lessons you remember or quotes they used over and over. Don't forget to note spiritual lessons and habits passed down. If you are a parent or grandparent, what do you hope your children and grandchildren would write? Spend some time thinking, praying and writing of the generational faith in your family and how you can ensure it is passed on.

DAY 31 - PROCLAIM

Psalm 71:17-18

*"O God, from my youth you have taught me, and I still
proclaim your wondrous deeds. So even to old age and gray
hairs, O God, do not forsake me, until I proclaim your might
to another generation, your power to all those who come."*

Stereotypically getting old comes with many challenges. I
say "stereotypically" because there are some people who seem
to have gained access to the mythical fountain of youth, staying
active, fit, and engaged well into their 80's and 90's. But generally
speaking, getting older sets in motion a whole host of physical
and mental realities. Eyesight fades. It's harder to hear (I said, "It's
harder to hear"). A good night's sleep is elusive. Afternoon naps
become necessary. Backs ache. Hair gets gray or leaves all together.
Old injuries predict the weather. Bones become brittle. Walking
becomes a challenge. Strength fades. Thought processes slow.
Where was I? Cold weather seems colder. Careers come to an end.
Culture and technology pass us by.

If you are an older reader, please don't be offended or depressed.
There is a point to be made here. I'm not trying to discourage
you by making you aware of your limitations, rather I desire to
encourage you to see past the realities of aging to embrace the

contributions only you can make. If you're younger, there are two reasons you should not skip today's reading: 1). No matter how young and invincible you now seem to be, you too will one day grow old. 2). The older generation has something you need that only they can provide.

The lyrics we have read today from "Song 71" in the ancient Jewish hymnbook is a worship song that seems to have been written by an older person of faith. Psalm 71:9 may reveal the author's physical age and perhaps his state of mind: "Do not cast me off in the time of old age; forsake me not when my strength is spent." We can't say for sure who wrote these words because the composer is not identified. But many scholars have attributed this song to David because it sounds like some of the other lyrics he penned. If it was David, he may be recalling victorious charges he once led into battle, how he fiercely protected his sheep from a lion, or how he once killed the Philistine champion. But now, at the end of his life, he didn't ride into battle any more. He was too old and slow to kill a lion. And arthritis in his shoulder prevented him from using his sling shot. What good is an old king in the kingdom of God?

Some of us older Christians can relate to this chorus. Now that we're older, we resonate with the words "cast off" and "forsake" because it feels like our family, our culture, the workforce, younger generations, and maybe even our church have set us aside. We once led the church and were the energy behind her mission. We prayed for God's miraculous hand to deliver and witnessed the answer to those prayers. We had ideas on how we could be more winsome in our witness. We crafted vision statements that inspired and organized growth strategies that were quite effective. But now, no one seems to be asking our opinion any more. Maybe we should be bold enough to invite someone younger than us into our circle. Maybe young people are more receptive than we had imagined and we're all missing out.

Some of us younger Christians should consider the words of this chorus as well. As young adults or students have we "cast off" and "forsaken" those who have gone before us and laid the foundation upon which we build? This is not a guilt trip. Most of us have not literally or intentionally told the older people in our lives to "take a hike." Still, we tend to inadvertently cast off the elderly because they can't keep up with the frantic pace of our youth. Maybe we should slow down long enough to at least ask the question, "What do older people know that I don't?" Maybe we should be bold enough to ask an older Christian to invest in a mentoring relationship. Maybe we should invite them into our planning and slow down long enough to listen to what they have to say.

As both young and old generations consider the questions posed above, let's review together our verses for today and discover what old age and gray hairs have to offer and how younger generations can encourage and receive that offering.

Older generations lead the praise. Psalm 71:8 says, "My mouth is filled with your praise, and with your glory all the day." It is crucial that older generations participate in the weekly corporate worship services of the local body so that they can lead by example in the spiritual discipline of praising God. While I know that church music styles have changed, the message and lyrics have not. God is worthy of praise, and those who have been around the longest in church should be the ones most inclined to sing praises because they have proven his greatness over and over. What if older generations made a point of singing out, shouting "hallelujah," raising hands, and clapping during the weekly assembly so that younger ones could see their praise? And what if a younger generation noticed? There is no greater testimony than boldly proclaiming God's glory and the older generation can lead the way on this. Speaking of testimonies:

Older generations have longer testimonies. I'm not talking about "long" in the sense of droning on and on in a boring way, but "long" as in more years of experiencing his work in their lives.

Psalm 71:15 says, "My mouth will tell of your righteous acts, of your deeds of salvation all the day, for their number is past my knowledge." If God is a God of salvation (and he is) and if God is a God miracles (and he is), then it makes sense for someone who has followed him for decades to have a longer testimony than one who is younger. Here the Psalmist says that he can't even number the righteous acts of God in his life. Sadly, there are many great stories of faith that are never shared with a younger generation. Please take time now to get involved in an area of ministry that will position you next to younger people in the church. Sign up to serve, go on a mission trip, be a part of a ministry team. Don't allow your lack of involvement be the reason your story never gets heard. Young adults and students, get close to older generations intentionally by inviting them to your small group or home and let them share their story.

Older generations are vital to legacy. As we consider legacy, the heaviest responsibility falls on the older ones among us. May the older generations (and only the youngest among us don't have a generation we're older than) embody the passion and prayer of our verse today. Let's ask God to allow us to share our faith so that the generations behind us can bear the torch of the church to the generations behind them. Make this verse your prayer today: God, "so even to old age and gray hairs [let us] proclaim your might to another generation." Amen.

What is your story? How are you sharing with a generation younger than you? How are you learning from a generation older than you are? Seriously. Think about it. Do something.

DAY 32 - WE ARE FAMILY

Ephesians 6:1-4

"Children, obey your parents in the Lord, for this is right. 'Honor your father and mother' (this is the first commandment with a promise), 'that is may go well with you and that you may live long in the land.' Fathers do not provoke your children to anger, but bring them up in the discipline and instruction of the Lord"

WARNING: Today's reading may cause deep conviction inspiring change to become the family member God designed you to be.

Dad is impatiently weaving through daily traffic as he heads home after a long day at work. Details and interactions race through his mind, but none like the conversation he had with his supervisor. "After all these years, could they be terminating my job?" He mused. The drive home soon turned into a driveway obstacle course of bikes, bats, and sidewalk chalk, but he finally managed his way into the garage. He was greeted with the faint voice of his wife from a darkened living room where after a day of chasing three kids around, she lay with a migraine. She apologized for not having dinner. He too was exhausted, but graciously asked if he could do anything for her.

Before she could answer, a loud thud that seemed to shake the house preceded the youngest, eight year old Ella, bounding down the stairs screaming and holding her bloody nose. Behind her, two older brothers entered, each yelling over the other about how their sister got hurt. Mom is motionless. Baby girl is hurting. Boys are being boys. Dad has had it... and explodes. In a flurry of regretful eloquence, he angrily yells at both boys grounding them to their room, reprimands his daughter for being a baby and demands that she stop crying. And for good measure, he mutters just loud enough for his wife to hear, "I guess you're gonna lay there." She tearfully responds, "Why are you being so mean? Why don't you just go back to work?" as she heads to the bedroom closing the door. How did this safe haven called home and God's gift of family so quickly turn to chaos?

With a few details changed here and there, this imaginary story could take place in any one of our houses. Your home may have fewer children, older children, or grandchildren. You may be a single parent, have a blended family, be newlyweds with no kids, or have grown children living with you. You may be an only child, one of eight, or somewhere in between. The truth is that home is the training ground for living out our faith. I guess this is why God placed commandment number five of the Big Ten (as quoted in our verse for the day) right in the middle of the commands guiding our relationship with him and others. Family is important to our spiritual formation – a holy legacy of sorts that we all are a part of, either good or bad. Whatever your family situation, a better family begins with you.

CHILDREN/STUDENTS. We'll begin where our verse begins, with two specific challenges for the children and students that make up the family. Before I dive in, a little admission about what I know: Parents aren't cool anymore (don't tell yours if they still think they are). Parents aren't always right (but it's hard to say it.) Parents love you more than you think. Parents know more than you think. Parents want the best for you. Parents often feel inadequate in their parenting and scared for how their kids will turn out. So, as a Christian student or child, you can help them by living out two commands.

Honor your parents. I have been around students long enough to know that some of you may be thinking, "What if my parents aren't honorable?" Let me give you three reasons you should honor your parents no matter what. 1) Your parents are made in the image of God and valuable to Him. He honors them as his creation. So should you. 2) God used your parents to bring you to life. Honor God's sovereignty in the parents he used to make you. 3) Your parents may have pain in their life you don't know about. Honor the fact that their parents weren't perfect either.

Obey. Most of the time, your parents' rules are not as dumb or unfair as you think they are. Just admit it. You, like all humans, just want to do things your way. Try to put yourselves in their shoes. I used to ask my sons, "If you were dad, what would your rules be?" The older you get, you'll find most (again not all, they aren't perfect) of their rules are in your best interest. Commit now to obey your parents. You won't regret it and you'll find them less stressed and more fun to be with.

PARENTS. Now for the parents in the family. Like it or not, God has placed you in a place of authority and responsibility. How you parent will most likely be the legacy of your family for generations to come. So don't blow this off. Pray about it. Work at it. Commit to it. There are three quick lessons from the Scriptures to consider here.

Model love and submission (Ephesians 5:21-25). Children thrive in a home where parents are in a loving, serving, and committed relationship under God's leadership. We don't have time here to expound the teaching from Ephesians 5 on marriage, but suffice it to say that when moms and dads model the love of Christ and the submission to one another, children see it and imitate it. The Christian life is about loving the other so much that you are willing to become a servant to them. If kids see parents putting the other first, they will learn to serve and love like this as well.

Sincere faith is copied faith (II Timothy 1:5). Like Timothy's sincere faith that he first saw in his mom and grandma, your child will imitate the faith they see in you. Don't focus on how to be a better parent as much as you focus on being a better Christ follower, because the bottom line is that your kids will nine times out of ten have the faith you have. Want your kids to pray? Pray. Want your kids to go to church? Go to church. Want your kids to love others? Love others. Want your kids to be generous? Be generous.

Educate, don't exasperate. Finally, we come to these two words pointed at dads, but applicable to mothers as well. "Do not provoke your children" and "...do not exasperate your children" (Colossians 3:21) are both challenges in Scripture because they are apparent challenges. Instead, parents are supposed to spend time instructing their children in the Lord. Why is this so hard? It's because parents are too busy. As parents, we must prioritize time to pray with our kids, read the Bible with our kids, and share our faith with our kids. Otherwise, our relationship will devolve into five minute, rule enforcing, one sided, authoritative speeches.

I sincerely believe that every member of the household can have significant influence on the home by aspiring to the godly roles outlined in the Bible. Would you prayerfully consider your place in your family and how you can make your home (no matter what it looks like) a place with a Christian legacy?

DAY 33 - CLOSE THE GAP

I Timothy 4:12

"Let no one despise you for your youth, but set the believers an example in speech, in conduct, in love, in faith, in purity."

"The children now love luxury; they have bad manners, contempt for authority; they show disrespect for elders and love chatter in place of exercise. Children are now tyrants, not the servants of their households. They no longer rise when elders enter the room. They contradict their parents, chatter before company, gobble up dainties at the table, cross their legs, and tyrannize their teachers." This quote is not an adult's indicting judgment on the youth and students of 21st century America. Instead, it is a quote attributed to the 4th century (B.C.) philosopher Socrates about the youth living in ancient Athens, Greece. I guess it's always been a challenge for older and younger generations to understand one another.

In the 1960's a term was created to describe this chasm between young and old; it was called a "generation gap." To be sure, every successive generation sees the world differently than the one before it because it grows up and is influenced by a totally different set of circumstances than the one before it. For example, the generation born to parents who experienced WWII grew up in a different America and therefore understand this country differently. In the same way, the current generation that was weaned on technology will never understand how the previous one survived without smart phones. They see the world differently as a result.

So it shouldn't be surprising to find a generation gap within the first century church at Ephesus. This seems to be what Paul is addressing to his "son in the faith" Timothy, who is the young pastor (think mid 30's) of this established and educated congregation. It's the word "despise" that gives us some insight into his struggle to be heard as a younger leader. The Greek word is "phroneo" and literally means "to think down." In other words, it appears some of the older generation in Timothy's church were in fact thinking or looking down on him because he was young. This does not appear to be an isolated incident, since Paul gives his other son in the faith, Titus the very same encouragement. "Let no one disregard (again "phroneo") you" (Titus 2:15).

Well, if older generations looked down on younger ones in the churches of Ephesus and in Crete, it's likely that the same thing is happening to some degree all these years later in your church. So what is a younger generation to do? Well if you are a kid or a student, let me begin with some scriptures Paul DIDN'T write to his young apprentice. "Let no one despise you for your youth. Demand your place around the table and tell them I said so" (III Timothy 3:1); or "Let no one despise you for your youth, they're just a bunch of grouchy curmudgeons" (III Timothy 2:1); or "Let no one despise you for your youth, take charge and kick out all who are against you; you are the pastor after all" (III Timothy 1:5). This is how "not to" when it comes to closing the generation gap and making a difference in your church. So what does he say?

First of all, I hope no one tried to look up scriptures from III Timothy; the book doesn't exist. Second, if you are young, let your generational focus in the church be this one word that Paul encourages in Timothy. If you're old like me, the word and everything else in this reading applies to all Christians, but I'm directing this word to the students. The best way young people can make a difference in their church is by "example." That's what Paul is telling you. Set an example. This is yet another cool word from the original Bible language. It is the word "tupos." We get our word "type" from it and it literally means the strike or impression a chisel made on stone as letters were carved into it. You can probably ask your parents about a thing called a "typewriter"- a device that left a mark every time you hit the key for that letter. An example is to leave a mark or impression and Paul says the best thing a young person can do is leave a mark by his or her example. Consider these five ways you can make an impression in your church (in spite of your age) by simply being an example.

Speech

The words that come out of our mouths can either be sweet like honey or taste bitter as contaminated water and though the tongue is hard to tame, we get to choose. Set an example to every generation in your church by using words that inspire and encourage; eliminate ones that are crude and filled with gossip. Try speaking with respect, joy, and complete sentences to an adult near you. It will make a great impression.

Conduct

Another way to influence everyone around you is to live a life in which others see Jesus. Yes, being young is a time where having fun sometimes clouds the judgment, so ask the Holy Spirit to keep you from the things this world "expects" of kids your age. Set an example by fully engaging in the worship and activities of the church. For starters, allow older adults to see you praying, reading your Bible, and greeting others with a Christian hug. Today's younger generations should be aware more than any before that someone is watching you all the time. What does your life say? It speaks louder than any word.

Love

This challenge may be the greatest of all, because we're talking about giving the love that you have received from Jesus to those around you. In our church we call it "ridiculous love" because the unmerited love and favor God has for us is just crazy. But it's true nonetheless. So set an example in your church by following three simple scriptures. Love one another (John 13:34). Attract others to Jesus by loving those in the church well. Love your enemies (Matthew 5:44). Literally imitate God's love by caring for those who don't like you. Love your neighbor as yourself (Mark 12:31). Jesus said this is the second greatest command and one that will help you influence your church. Work at thinking about and meeting the needs of those around you.

Faith

Set an example by demonstrating that you truly believe Jesus to be your Lord and Savior. You can do this by verbally sharing your testimony, or you can demonstrate it in tangible ways. The best opportunity for displaying your faith as a young person comes mostly in times that cause students and young adults to despair. When you don't make the team, experience a break up, don't get the scholarship, or experience a tragedy, what do you really believe about Jesus? The answer to that question and your response based on that belief will be more influential than any one thing you can do.

Purity

Finally, keep yourself pure by aggressively protecting your sexuality. God made you (either male for female) for sexual expression, but specifically in the context of marriage. As a young person, this culture bombards you with sexual images and ideologies. Set an example to every generation in your church by living a life that recognizes, avoids, and quickly repents of sin. Let these words that Jesus taught become a daily prayer, "Lead us not into temptation, but deliver us from the evil one" (Matthew 6:13).

DAY 34 - FAMILY TREE

I Timothy 5:1&2

"Do not rebuke an older man but encourage him as you would a father, younger men as brothers, older women as mothers, younger women as sisters, in all purity."

After 32 years of marriage, raising two boys, and seeing them into adulthood, there was still a familial relationship I had never experienced. But all of that changed within a period of six weeks in 2016. First, my oldest son Mikey was married to a lovely girl named Monica on Thanksgiving Eve and then on New Year's Eve, my youngest Caleb married the sweet and beautiful Jessica. Suddenly I had daughters and they have been one of the greatest blessings in my life. Boys are fun for wrestling and talking trash, but girls are sweet and have kind hearts. I love my boys, but these daughters – they are special.

All of us are a part of a family that by default exposes us to four basic God-designed relationships. These relationships are father, mother, brother, and sister. Of course, I am aware that not all families share the same family structure, but these are all relationships most of us can understand to some degree. I can say with full assurance, that every one of us has a mom and dad, and whether the relationship is good, bad, or broken, the parent-child dynamic is important. Most of us have also experienced growing up with a sibling or siblings, affording us the unique relationship between brothers and sisters. In one moment, we can be so frustrated we want to punch them and in the next, we can be so protective for their well-being. It's hard to explain, but brothers will physically fight with one another and for one another.

You may not have reflected on this reality before, but in the spiritual sense, we have way more family relationships than we may have realized. One of the blessings of being a Christ follower is that when you come to faith in Christ, you, like me with my new daughters, instantly gain a whole new set of relatives. In this letter, Paul has already reminded Timothy that we who are Christians are a part of "the household of God, which is the church of the living God" (I Timothy 3:15). And if this is God's house, then it obviously is made up of the usual roles associated with home and family; namely, our spiritual fathers, mothers, brothers and sisters of faith who make up our local church.

Fathers

Paul first tells Timothy that he should approach the older men in the congregation as if they were his father. Two simple pieces of advice for dealing with fathers: Don't rebuke them. Encourage them. Because of the male ego, I've not met many men (old or otherwise) who respond well to public and/or harsh comments directed their way. The first instinct is to defend and fight back. So instead, Paul says that children in the church should "encourage" as you would a father. This familiar New Testament word ("parakaleo") means to call to one's side.

We are at our best with the old men, fathers, and grandfathers in our church when they know we are on their side. As children, the best thing we can do for a father is to let them know how much we appreciate them for all they've done for us and let them know we rely on their wisdom and strength. This is true for both physical and spiritual fathers. Along with this, a challenge to old men seems appropriate. Embrace the children of the congregation. What an opportunity we have to influence the two or three (four?) generations after us for Jesus. Paul was quite aware of his parenting role, referring to both Timothy and Titus as his children in the faith (I & II Timothy, Titus 1:4).

Mothers

Along with the fathers in the church, we are also reminded that we have faith moms. Again, not all moms are alike, but most moms have a gentle and caring way about them. At least when I was growing up, I would go to mom when I was hurting. I knew dad would just tell me to "shake it off" and "be strong," but mom would care enough to hold me and kiss my "ouchy" until it was better. Of course, I've seen this same thing in my wife as the mother of my boys. As they have gotten older, their "ouchies" have changed, but they will still turn to mom for a softer, gentler response.

How blessed the church is to have great women of faith who care, pray, and serve in a way that only moms do. Don't get me wrong, men are caring and women are strong and wise, but when I need prayer, encouragement, or some tender advice, I go to a spiritual mom every time. Older women, consider the children of the congregation as your very own and nurture them as only you can.

Brothers

Paul also gives advice for how Timothy (and we) should approach those guys in the congregation who are younger men, and closer to our age. The term "brothers" is used 224 times in the New Testament, and most of the time it is in reference to other men in the body of Christ. In our vernacular, we might call them "bros" or "dudes" but young guys in the church are there for strength. You can count on them for shooting straight in conversation as well as being there to defend their siblings. In our tradition, it was common to refer to other men in the church by combining the word "brother" and their last name (e.g. brother Baker). We don't do that as much anymore, but maybe we should because the church is made up of some good "bros."

Sisters

The last segment of family to address is the sisters in the congregation. We can name at least two of Paul's sisters in the faith because he recognized and mentioned them in his writings: "...our sister Phoebe..." (Romans 16:1), "...Apphia our sister..." (Philemon 1:2). Here he gives a qualification for living with sisters, and that is "with all purity." Our young sisters in the congregation may be outwardly beautiful but they are equally as strong in faith and wisdom as their brothers. They bring a loving and tender aspect to the church that is invaluable. Younger women are not fragile, but they are usually more delicate. Pay attention to your sisters in Christ for they regularly display the meekness of Christ. Pray for them and care for them as sisters.

In your story for this week, spend some time considering who your spiritual parents are. Also, spend some time considering your spiritual siblings. Name those brothers and sisters in Christ who push you, influence you, and love you. For those who are older, you may also wish to write down some spiritual children of the faith. Like the apostle Paul, of whom would you say, "my child in the faith?" Don't skip this important exercise. In essence, you are identifying your church family tree. Thank God for your spiritual family today.

DAY 35 - GLORIOUS HERITAGE

Ephesians 3:20&21

"Now to him who is able to do far more abundantly than all we ask or think, according to his power within us, to him be glory in the church and in Christ Jesus throughout all generations, forever and ever. Amen."

Like never before, it seems that Americans have a passionate interest in origins. Perhaps the pace of life, separation from family (both geographic and literal), and an increased feeling of groundlessness have caused millions to learn about their past. We believe that by discovering where we come from and who our relatives are, we may gain some real insights into who we are. This is why websites like "Ancestry.com" and "23andme.com" have literally exploded on the scene for a culture clamoring for connection to its past.

Several years ago, before the internet was commonplace and these tools of discovery existed, my sister Angie decided to do some research on our family. After a year or so, she shared her findings, giving us some great insight into our family tree. It was exciting to find names from generations past that were shared with us or our children. It was interesting to find out about the moves, the

146

hardships, and the fortunes of ancestors long past. It was almost validating to find where our family, at least partially, originated. On my paternal grandmother's side of the family, my sister traced our heritage back to the Von Questenburg family in 14th century Germany. Sounds fancy. For some reason, this discovery made me proud and gave me a sense of belonging.

Proud of a rich Christian past.

One of the more interesting (and humbling) parts of tracing your family roots is that you find you are related to some unsavory characters. For example, some discover bank robbers, slave owners, swindlers, and worse (Al Capone and Hitler in someone's family tree!) Along with negative family realities, we find pain. We find out great grandma's mom died when she was three, or three of the eleven children in one family died before age two, or a great uncle took his life when his family lost the farm. There really are no exceptions. Every family tree has its share of villainy and pain. Our goal is not to be that guy or gal for future generations.

The generations of family that make up the church is no different. In 2,000 years there have been some embarrassing moments and things done in the name of Jesus that make us wince and cry. The crusades during the years of 1096-1221 A.D. are a part of our heritage that we wish were not there. But in fact, the cross was emblazoned on the shields and men killed in the name of Jesus. Closer to home, we know that during the American slavery period, we know that people found in the churches' family tree enslaved men and women who were treated as non-persons. I don't like that part of my Christian history, but it is there nonetheless. When people ask me as a pastor about these, and other major tragedies and sins in our spiritual family, I remind them of two things. 1) The church is of necessity imperfect because it has always been made up of people and people are imperfect. 2) Not all things done in the name of Jesus represented the true family of Jesus.

On the other side of the discovery of our roots, we have the triumph of Christ's worldwide church. Throughout the generations since its inception in Acts 2, the church has prevailed. As Jesus predicted, the gates of hell have not been able to stand against the church and it has been and still is the most influential force in the world today. Consider the sheer spiritual force of billions who have come to faith in Christ in two millennia. And then, celebrate all the practical healing the church has brought to the world in that time. Our Christian ancestors broke down the racial and sexist inequities in first century Rome by including all. Good men and women of our faith campaigned to abolish slavery, rescue kids from the factories, start schools for the poor, establish hospitals for healing, establish rescue organizations, and create social change agencies. Red Cross? Christian. Good will? Christian. Salvation Army? Christian. Samaritan's Purse and Compassion International? Christian. World, national, and local responders in emergencies and crisis? Largely churches and Christian organizations. What a great heritage we have. May future generations come behind us and find us to be world changers for him.

Belonging to a glorious Christian future.

But, as our Scripture today indicates, we are not only a church of the past; we have a glorious future. While it is impossible to tell how long it will be before Jesus comes to take his bride home, we know that until that designated "Day of the Lord," the church will continue. Practically, this means that no matter what generation we are in right now, the generation after us, and the one after them, and the 10 that follow them, will carry on the message and mission of the church of Jesus Christ. He will be glorified in the world and he has raised up future spiritual relatives to follow in our footsteps. Even now, there are unborn children… future relatives of ours who will preach the gospel, serve in Jesus' name, travel to other cultures, and give their lives for the cause of Christ.

Then, some sweet day, we'll all meet in glory for the biggest family reunion in history. And there, around the glorious feast called the "wedding of the Lamb," our eternal Father will recount the story of our family. And we will celebrate our heritage, forever and ever. Why wouldn't we start that celebration today?

DAY 36 - REST

Joshua 24:32

"As for the bones of Joseph, which the people of Israel brought up from Egypt, they buried them at Shechem, in the piece of land that Jacob bought from the sons of Hamor the father of Shechem for a hundred pieces of money. It became an inheritance of the descendants of Joseph."

When I was a kid, I enjoyed grade school. Didn't mind math or English. Really liked socializing with classmates in general. Loved the play of recess and the food at lunch. And, with the exception of third grade (Miss Tackett – long story) I liked all of my teachers. Honestly, there was only one part of my early primary education that I didn't care for. Rest period. This was a 15-20 minute time of rest that was built into the schedule of every day. At the beginning of the school year, children brought their own carpet square that was stacked neatly in the corner of the classroom. Then at the appointed time each day, every child retrieved their mat, put it on the floor, and lay down (a variation was laying your head on your desk). The teacher turned the lights off with instruction that there should be no talking, no looking around, no moving – in other words no fun. Boooooooring! All these years later, I've come to appreciate the gift and spiritual discipline of rest even if I'm not always consistent in practicing it.

As we come to the end of our Joshua 24 experience, you may think that rest is a really strange way to end a study that has encouraged spiritual experience and action, but this is how the book of Joshua ends. In the most anticlimactic of ways, the book of Joshua ends by giving us the burial details of two famous guys. First, Joseph, prince of Egypt, favorite son of Jacob, and father to two Israelite tribes (Manasseh and Ephraim) finally has his bones laid to rest in the family tomb. Second, Eleazar, the high priest and son of the first high priest, Aaron, was buried in the hill country of Ephraim. The casual Bible reader may be tempted to think, "Who cares?" But, these details are not just insignificant ancient obituaries, a sort of appendix to the exciting story of conquest. Instead they are part of the written, and powerful, and "breathed out" word of God and as such are "profitable" (II Timothy 3:16).

We would profit to learn that rest is a part of our earthly experience and a picture of the rest that awaits us all in the end. Conventional wisdom on how many hours of sleep we need each night varies, but most experts land somewhere between 7-9 hours. While individual needs can vary slightly, it is something that one cannot do without. It is very human to sleep. Have you ever thought about the implications of God's design for our rest? He created humans to spend eight hours out of every 24-hour cycle resting. In other words, one third of our entire life-on-earth experience should be sleep. The reason so many of us are exhausted and stressed is that we believe we are the exception to this eternal rule of rest that God designed for our lives. This sleep is necessary and also a picture of the rest that awaits us all in death.

When someone is buried, a common sentiment (and often tombstone inscription) is "rest in peace." Why do we say that? We use this expression because death is a symbol of rest after a lifelong journey of trials and toils; relationships gained and lost, victories and defeats, and celebrations and mourning. When taken all at once, this lifetime of experiences seems tiring and calls for rest. Death is a sort of rest at the end, a final resting place (another phrase we use to speak of someone's burial location) of a lifetime of experiences.

The burial of Joseph represents the resting place of some long and often difficult circumstances. In Genesis, chapters 37-50 we see the incredible story of Joseph who was at varying points in his life a favorite son, a hated and abused brother, enslaved in Egypt, falsely accused of adultery, imprisoned, forgotten, given the ability to interpret dreams, raised to the throne, manager of a world famine, and rescuer of his family. His is literally a rags to riches story, but even with his success in Egypt, he longed for rest. In the very last verse of Genesis, he predicts that God would surely visit the sons of Israel in the future and made them swear, "You shall carry up my bones from here" (Genesis 50:28). According to Egyptian custom, they embalmed him upon his death and the people of God carried his coffin around for 500 years until they burned him. Rest after a long life.

Eleazar is no different. While we don't have the detail of his life that we do for Joseph, we know that he was appointed as the second High Priest of God when his father, the original high priest died. In this scene, Moses actually took the official priestly garments off Aaron on Mt. Hor and placed them on Eleazar. Shortly after this Aaron died and Israel mourned (see Numbers 20:22-29). What a surreal way to get a promotion. Simultaneously weeping over his father's death and feeling the weight of his new role. This is not to mention the trauma he had witnessed that led to him being the high priest in the first place. Being the third son of Aaron, he wasn't in line to become the high priest. It surely would have gone to his older brothers, Nadab and Abihu. However, in Leviticus 10 we're told that God struck them down for profaning his tabernacle by burning strange incense on the altar. As part of the judgement, the family was told not to mourn! Though they had sinned, he must have felt pain at his brothers' death. So, when we get to this burial at the end of Joshua, it represents rest at the end of the journey.

We are a lot like Joseph and Eleazar. On our lifelong journeys through this world, most of us have experienced betrayal like Joseph. In addition, even though most of us are not high priests or princes, we like both Eleazar and Joseph have experienced successful moments along the way. Each of us has or will face the pain of a loved one's death. There will be times when our respective positions and roles in this world are tiresome and even overwhelming. We all experience family issues, great and small. We get up every day to a world filled with the wonder of God and the disobedient influence of sin. Life is both a great blessing, and yet very tiring. You may not have thought about your death in this way before, but it is the rest from this life that we all are longing for.

In the meantime, God loves us so much that he has given us commands about rest. These are not for him. They are for us, because he designed our bodies and knows our lives inside and out. And, he desires rest for us. Unfortunately, we live in a world that pays less attention to rest than ever before and we are paying the price for it. While we may not be called to a ritual observance of the Sabbath (Hebrew "Shabbat" – to cease) we are called to relax as a part of the rhythm of life. A friend once pointed out that when it comes to resting we should "divert daily, withdrawal weekly, and retreat regularly." It's good advice for the Christ following life we aspire to. So let me encourage you to assess your rest as you look forward to that final and eternal rest.

On the page provided below write down your current patterns of rest. If you aren't getting enough sleep, take steps to get more. See a doctor if necessary. If you don't currently practice

Sabbath, make a commitment to make regular rest a priority. If your schedule is too hectic, eliminate unnecessary activities and busyness. Spend sometime praying about this and commit to becoming a person of rest. Seriously. Chill. Rest. Sleep in. Take a nap. Relax. It may be the most spiritual thing you can do ahead of what God will do next in you. One last time, refer to the appropriate study guide in the back of this book for additional spiritual exercises during this week of rest.

Day 36 - Rest

DAY 37 - MORE REST

Exodus 34:21

"Six days shall you work, but on the seventh day you shall rest. In plowing time and harvest you shall rest."

My grandpa was old school and his faith was simple. By simple, I don't mean ignorant, because when I was a youth, he displayed that Indiana farmer common sense. It told you he understood a lot more than the knowledge you could find in books. He worked hard. Even in retirement, he and grandma (Loren and Lillian by name) maintained an acre (not exaggerating) of meticulously kept garden. Every summer my sister, brother, and I joined grandpa and grandma on the farm for a week. In my mind's eye, I can still see that garden with grandpa picking beans and digging up potatoes and grandma fussing with her flowers. As I recall, grandpa was in the garden after morning coffee and stayed there most days until the sun began its descent.

When it comes to hard, physical labor, my grandpa is still my standard of what it means to put in an "honest day's work." However, I never (and I mean never) saw my grandpa work on Sunday. On Sunday his clothes changed, usually from overalls to slacks with a jacket. After breakfast, he read the paper or the Bible. By 8:30 am or so, we were headed to Sunday school at 9:00

am, followed by church at 10:30 am. Then we went home and had lunch. And then, grandpa did nothing. He reclined in his chair and took naps. He sat on the porch and drank lemonade in the cool of the evening. He ate popcorn with the family as we sat in the living room watching television together. He never did a thing on Sundays. The Lord's Day was, for him, a sacred day of rest and he allowed nothing to encroach upon that Sabbath.

In his original meeting with God on the mountain, Moses received what we commonly refer to as the Ten Commandments. This meeting and these commandments are recorded for us in Exodus 20. We have already discussed them in this book in chapter three. There we noted that God calls us to rest. "Remember the Sabbath day, to keep it holy" is the way he says it in Exodus 20:8. So why are we returning to this topic of rest? I'll get to that in just a minute, but first a question for you, dear reader. In the 34 days since the reading on day three, have you taken tangible steps to make rest a regular rhythm of your life? I ask, not because I doubt you specifically, but because I know humans all too well. I'm guessing that you, like me, continue to struggle with this rest thing. So let's dig a little deeper into Sabbath.

The reason we have our verse from today is because the people of God broke the Ten Commandments before Moses could even get down from the mountain to share them. In his righteous indignation, Moses threw down the two tablets requiring him to make another visit to the holy mountain. When Moses arrived with the new stones, God didn't say, "Okay, Big Mo, let's just go with six commandments, maybe ten was too much." If anything, God expanded the laws by giving more insight into the covenant he was entering into with his people. And while he doesn't actually talk about the Sabbath day specifically, he uses the Hebrew word for rest, the word "sha bat" twice. It is as if God is saying, "My Sabbath Day is sacred whether you obey it or not; but let me explain it a little more."

158

This brings me back to my grandpa and his habit of doing nothing but worship on Sundays. I think the lessons we need to reconsider from this one verse are profound and ones that my grandpa figured out.

Rest is just as important as your work.

God thinks work is important. In fact, it was his work that got this whole world and the human-being thing started. There is no harder worker than God. I know, I know, that sounds funny. After all, he is God. How hard is it to create the starry universe? Can't he just say the word and form oceans, mold mountains, and carve valleys? Was it really that difficult to scoop up some mud and form Adam? If God is as powerful as we understand him to be, then what does it mean for him to work? Can't he just snap his fingers and it is done? Well, yes. But still the Bible says, "...on the seventh day God finished his work that he had done..." The word for the work associated with God in this verse means "business" or "occupation." I bet you've never thought of God having a job but we should, because all things God are implanted in those of us who are made in his image.

So work is important. He is all for a six day workweek. God knows we can find pleasure and joy in working to create and sustain projects. He knows we find purpose in progress and satisfaction in building, planning, and organizing. It's just that he thinks rest is equally as important. God is telling us that a seven-day workweek is not more productive than working six days. If you want a productive work life... if you want to accomplish a lot in life... if you want to get that project done... if you want to graduate from college... a weekly rest day is the way to go. I've led staff members before with this line: "You may be exceptional, but you're not the exception." If God takes a rest day, then so should you. He is just as pleased when you rest in him as when you work for him.

Rest is not to be ignored during busier seasons.

The second lesson to be learned from God's expounding of the Sabbath Day law, is that he realizes there are some seasons in life busier than others. To the mostly agrarian congregation in the time of Moses, the yearly rhythms of plowing and harvest represented times of increased work in the fields. The temptation would be to skip the Sabbath because there was still so much land to be planted in the spring, or to put in seven days of work to make sure the harvest was completed in the fall. God, however, commands that even during these hectic, busy, and stressful times of production, his people are still called to rest in him.

Though most of us aren't farmers any more, the Sabbath still applies no matter how busy the season is. These days we are tempted to skip rest to study for finals, to prepare for the annual report, or to clean the house for the holidays. We work seven days in a row to finish the school project. We say yes to "over time" in order to make more money during the holidays. We take second jobs to send our kids to college. Never separated from our jobs, we manage to work on our "day off" to clear all the emails from our iPhones. We talk about, "when things slow down" but continue to pack our calendars with social events, work meetings, kids' events, and travel. God says, "Stop, cease, pause, Sabbath." We're exhausted as a result. We have convinced ourselves that we can live 24/7 lives when God specifically designed us for 18/6 ones.

One last time before we end this experience together: isn't it time for us to do something about this obvious Christian discipline that most of us are mishandling? Think about it. Pray about it. Do something with your schedule.

DAY 38 - EASY

Matthew 11:28-30

"Come to me, all who labor and are heavy laden, and I will give you rest. Take my yoke upon you, and learn from me, for I am gentle and lowly in heart, and you will find rest for your souls. For my yoke is easy, and my burden is light."

I guess we've all seen enough television shows depicting the life of a doctor to know that one of the major pitfalls of the medical profession is lack of sleep. This is especially true in the world of medical residents. These people have graduated from medical school, but continue to learn for three years under supervising doctors. According to regulations, these residents may work up to 80 hours a week, which may include shifts of up to 30 hours at a time! So these are the people who drink that terrible hospital coffee?! These may be some of the most "under-rested" people in our world and they often maintain this exhausting schedule for years.

As Jesus speaks to the crowds in the book of Matthew, he notices something about them that resembles medical residents. They are tired. Exactly whom he's talking to and what kind of tired he is talking about has been debated for decades. My understanding is that he sees a bunch of people who are seeking God, but looking in all of the wrong places. Instead of noticing the works that he is doing as a fulfillment of God's law delivered through Moses, they are missing it completely. They are working hard at carrying the religion of their fathers, but they are missing the heart of God. They are trying to be spiritual, but they are failing and they are exhausted trying.

This is what Jesus notices when he makes his great invitation to come to him. He is inviting those who "labor" – a Greek word (kopiao) that means "grow weary, tired or exhausted from physical work." He is also inviting those that are heavy laden, a term that simply is "to feel the weight of something heavy laid upon" them. Of course, this exhaustion applies to all of our tiredness which is why most of us read this verse with delight. Wouldn't it be great if someone could help lift some of the weight off our shoulders? Wouldn't it be nice to be well rested deep within our souls? Wouldn't it be great to learn a new and easier way? Well, Jesus is that way and today he invites us to lighten our load.

OPTION ONE: Heavy laden religion

Trying to be perfect is heavy. But that's what Jesus has already taught in Matthew 5:48, "You therefore must be perfect, as your Heavenly Father is perfect." Of course, God is perfect. He is complete. Nothing needs to be added. He is as good as good gets. We, on the other hand, are not perfect and even defend ourselves with the phrase, "nobody's perfect." Hold on to this call for us to be perfect; we'll get back to that in just a minute. The point is that many of us have spent, or are spending our lives trying to impress God by being "good."

Trying to convince everyone else you're perfect is exhausting. Another burden of religion is that we are constantly working at making everyone else think we are perfect. This was the aim of the religious leaders, dressing the part, saying the right words, and showing themselves in public worship. But their hypocritical hearts were far from God. We are tempted to do the same. We put on our Christian best on Sundays or around other Christians. We talk about our prayer times, our Bible study, and our clean living while hiding the sins we struggle with. We carry the heavy weight of hiding our true selves from others, and in the meantime load them down with the guilt of not being as good as we are. Heavy indeed.

Multiplying rules just get heavier. As most of us know, God started with essentially ten laws. These rules given to Moses on the mountain ended up being 613 rules in the Talmud (the collection of Jewish writings to expound on the Moses' teachings) as taught by the Jewish rabbis. In other words, the heavy burden of first knowing and then following all the rules was placed on a people searching for God. In some way, we do the same thing in the 21st century church, imposing our understanding of Christ following on others. This may be anything from rules on dating, schooling, dress, media, and the use of alcohol. It seems there is no end to the list of rules we come up with to keep ourselves (and others) in line.

Constant weight of failure. The heaviest part of all is dealing with our realizations of how short we fall of perfection and how guilty that makes us feel. Don't get me wrong, we do fail and when we do, we should feel guilty. But we've got guilt all wrong. Guilt is a gift from God designed to help us know that we have done wrong and to call us back to him and his ways. Guilt is not designed for us to carry; for when we do it's heavy.

OPTION TWO: The light load of Jesus' grace

Rest in his grace. Notice that Jesus is not saying you don't have to carry some weight in this world. He too calls us to follow the ways of God. He believes in every law Moses ever delivered. He commands us to obey his teachings. When he says, "take my yoke upon you," it is a calling with weight to it, but it's not as heavy as religion. He comes to fulfill the law by showing us the grace of God the law was designed to inspire in humankind. God desires relationship, not law-following. So he came in the flesh to forgive our sin and give us what we could never achieve on our own – sinlessness. He does this by taking our sin and nailing it to a cross. Rest in this today. You are under his grace.

Rest in authenticity. This grace allows us to be authentic in the body of Christ. Since I know you are a sinner saved by grace, and you know I'm a sinner saved by grace; we can honestly confess our sins, share our struggles, love one another, and offer grace to all. Church should be the most low-pressure environment in the world. There is nothing to brag about except the work of the Lord's grace (I Corinthians 1:31). There is nothing to hide because we are all in this together and have come from the same place. There is nothing to prove, because none of us could save ourselves. Relax. Be yourself. You're in the company of the redeemed.

Rest in second chances. We can rest in the fact that in Christ we are forgiven and by his grace allowed to move forward in grace. I'm so glad it's not "three strikes and you're out" with God. I'm blessed that God is a not a pass/fail grade. We can rest in Jesus today because the one who died for us knows us best and still died for us. His forgiveness is ongoing. "If we confess our sin, he is faithful and just to forgive us our sin and cleanse us from all unrighteousness" (I John 1:9).

Rest in formation. This brings us back to that call to perfection we looked at above. The word for "perfect" in the language of the Bible means "complete." Being perfect is not the exhausting pursuit of sin free living, but the burden-lifting following of the one who has freed my life from sin. I can live perfect because that is the end of my story. "And I am sure of this, that he who began a good work in you will bring it to completion at the day of Jesus Christ" (Philippians 1:6). How easy could it be? We trust him. He takes our sin. We walk with him. He makes us perfect.

DAY 39 - COME AWAY

Mark 6:30-31

"The apostles returned to Jesus and told him all that they had done and taught. And he said to them, "Come away by yourselves to a desolate place and rest a while."

Obviously, I love Jesus for all the spiritual things he has done for me that only he could do. Among these are forgiveness and remission of my sin, overcoming my death, filling me with his Spirit, and giving me eternal hope. I could go on. But I also love the human side we see in Jesus because it reminds me that aside from saving me, he also understands me. As a guy with an appetite, I'm glad Jesus got hungry and ate with friends. He was hungry when he looked for fruit on the fig tree (Mark 11:12) and again after had risen from the dead he asked, "Have you anything here to eat?" (Luke 24:41). Jesus' tears also warm my heart. In Scripture we find him weeping at a friend's funeral (John 11:35) and crying for the holy city Jerusalem (Luke 19:41). I'm grateful that he had friends. He truly enjoyed company with Mary, Martha, and Lazarus ("he whom you love is ill" John 11:3) and of course, he called his apostles his friends (John 15:15).

I could go on, but there's one more thing I really love about Jesus – like me and you he got tired. God, dressed in human flesh felt the reality of fatigue, exhaustion, sleeplessness, and weariness. You may remember the story about Jesus and the woman at the well, but do you remember how he met her? "Jesus, wearied as he was from his journey, was sitting beside the well" (John 4:6). In Luke 9:58 he gives a would-be follower insight into his weary world remarking that, "the Son of Man [Jesus] has nowhere to lay his head" (Luke 9:58). Of course, the greatest insight into just how much exhaustion Jesus experienced comes from the story of him calming the wind and the waves. "And behold, there arose a great storm on the sea, so that the boat was being swamped by the waves; but he was asleep" (Matthew 8:24). Do you know how tired you have to be to sleep through the drenching he received in the back of this fishing boat? Jesus understood what it meant to be physically tired. And so he recommended rest for his closest followers.

Our verse for the day comes in the context of Mark 6 where we find some energy draining events that lead to Jesus' invitation. First, he is rejected in his hometown by those he grew up with and knew the best (Mark 6:1-6). Next, he sends his twelve closest friends on a ministry tour of Galilee. Two by two, these men walked from town to town, preached Jesus, healed people, and cast out demons (Mark 6:7-12). Finally, Jesus heard of the death of his relative and ministry partner, John the Baptist (Mark 7:13-29). In these short 29 verses, we find three tiring circumstances. Rejection of others was emotionally exhausting. The work of ministry was physically and spiritually tiring. The tragedy of death was spiritually tiring. So, when the Twelve return from their trip, he suggests some rest.

Do you need some rest? Are you tired from the difficulty of human relationships? It doesn't have to be rejection (although some of us likely have been by peers, boyfriends and girlfriends, spouses or employers). It can simply be the emotional strain of relationships in general. Perhaps you are tired from a long period of physical labor or an extra hectic time in your schedule. It seems to happen far too often these days. The calendar fills up and we find ourselves running from sun up to sun down. It's likely that some of us can relate to spiritual fatigue. Maybe you've experienced a death, a dry period in your small group, or the discouragement of seeing the ungodly prosper. For those of us who are tired in these and millions of other ways, Jesus' invitation still stands. Consider some rest with three simple spiritual disciplines Jesus offers his disciples, then and now.

Come away. True rest won't happen unless you come away. Jesus was inviting his followers to get away from the people-intensive ministry he had called them to. To rest, they needed to get away from all those requests for healing. They needed to retreat from the demands for casting out demons. The only way they would get refreshment was to be away from everything and everyone that may demand anything from them. For 21st century Christ followers, the call to come away remains. For most of us, this includes two simple (and strangely difficult) steps. First, we need to disconnect from all of our devices. There simply is no rest from texts, emails, alerts, tweets, and posts unless we intentionally power down and walk away. Second, we need to disconnect from the environment that made us tired in the first place. For stay at home moms, this may mean getting out of the house for a few hours. For students, get away from the dorm room, and for workaholics, get away from the office. Change of environment is the beginning of the rest Jesus desires for us.

Quiet place. The next consideration is destination. Jesus invites his followers to a "desolate place." The Greek word here is "heremos" and literally means "alone" or "solitary." It was often used synonymously with the desert, of which there was no shortage in the area surrounding the Sea of Galilee. Jesus knew that some time away in the quiet of God's creation would be just the thing for these weary servants. If you want to rest, find a quiet place. Go to a nearby lakefront. Drive out into the country. Sit under the shade of a tree in the local park. If you have a peaceful backyard, spend some time there. Or maybe you have a room in your house that is quiet. If you want to be more aggressive, take a few days to go the mountains, the ocean, or a retreat center. Whatever the location, make sure you are alone. Being alone naturally slows the pace and allows clearer thinking and praying.

Take Jesus with you. Finally, take Jesus with you. Of course, the apostles were blessed to be in the actual presence of their rabbi. Maybe they enjoyed some small talk and maybe they prayed together. Either way, the words of Jesus were clear and refreshing. My recommendation for taking Jesus with you is fourfold. First, invite your Lord, through his Holy Spirit, to speak to you. Second, take your Bible, pen, and notebook with you and just casually read some scriptures. Third, sit quietly and listen. Fourth, and finally, write down any inspirations you sense as you rest. You have just experienced the rest of a personal retreat with Jesus. Now, you can return to your family, your job, your school, and your life well rested.

DAY 40 - THE END

Hebrews 4:8-11

"For if Joshua had given them rest, God would not have spoken of another day later on. So then, there remains a Sabbath rest for the people of God, for whoever has entered God's rest has also rested from his works as God did from his. Let us therefore strive to enter that rest, so that no one may fall by the same sort of disobedience."

At the end, there is rest.
At the end of the semester, there is rest.
At the end of your career, there is rest.
At the end of a long day, there is rest.
At the end of the household chores, there is rest.
At the end of the sports season, there is rest.
At the end of the game, there is rest.
At the end of the marathon, there is rest.
At the end of the wedding planning, there is rest.
At the end of school assignments, there is rest.
At the end of the homework, there is rest.
At the end of a project, there is rest.
At the end of the yard work, there is rest.
At the end of the kids' bath and story time, there is rest.
At the end of holidays, there is rest.

At the end of the harvest season, there is rest.
At the end of the book of Joshua, there is rest.
At the end of this book, there is rest.
At the end of the Joshua 24 Experience, there is rest.
At the end of faith, there is rest.
At the end of the Jesus following life, there is rest.

Here at the end of our time with the Old Testament people of God in the book of Joshua we find them resting in the Promised Land. It has been a long, difficult, and dangerous journey. Following Joshua's lead, they have conquered the enemies of God that formerly occupied this land. They have divided the land as inheritances among the tribes, clans, and families of Israel. Nearly 600 years after the promise was made to Abraham, his descendants now occupy Canaan. As we noted in the first chapter, God said, "I gave you a land on which you had not labored and cities that you had not built, and you dwell in them. You eat the fruit of vineyards and olive orchards that you did not plant" (Joshua 24:13). For the people of Israel, there is nothing left to do, but relax and enjoy.

But as our verse on this final day of our experience teaches us, they had still not reached their final rest. Even though God had done everything he had promised, he still spoke of another day for the people of God where they would rest eternally. This may be shocking to those of us who look forward to heaven because it's not something we talk about a lot. We look forward to heaven as the wedding feast of the Lamb. We expectantly hope to see Jesus face to face. We anticipate walking on streets of gold and seeing the mansions Jesus has prepared for us. The prospect of standing before the throne of God in worship with people of every tribe, tongue, and nation is our future delight. But according to the writer of Hebrews, our eternity can best be seen as rest.

In this sense, we are a lot like our Hebrew brothers and sisters from long ago. While we have already received our inheritance in Jesus Christ, which is guaranteed by the presence of his Holy Spirit, we are not fully at rest here. While on earth, we still labor, live, learn, celebrate, mourn, plan, build, grow, play, and worship in this temporary Promised Land. This is not it. There is a rest for the people of God that awaits. Properly, heaven should be seen as a place where all fatigue, worry, stress, striving, busyness, exhaustion, and weariness have passed away. In other words, rest.

In the meantime, we practice at resting in Him. We rest in his love for us. We rest in the hope of this eternal rest. We rest in his forgiveness and removal of our sin. We rest in the power of His Spirit. We rest in his calling. We rest in family, the church. The more we learn to rest here, the more we get a taste of the rest there. So slow down. Take a deep breath. Stop over-scheduling. Take a nap on the couch. Sit and do nothing but listen. Kick back. Lie down. At the end of this experience, listen to the Holy Spirit. He's telling you to breathe.

Rest here.
Rest now.
Rest regularly.
Rest in Him.
Rest in his promises.
Rest in his word.
Rest in his grace.
Rest in his mercy.
Learn to rest now...
Because at the end, there is rest.

HOW TO USE THE
TENT EXPERIENCE

We learn more about God as we interact with those around us, in part, because their personal experiences produce a deeper expression of who God is and how He works intricately in and through us. That's why we are asking everyone to choose a "tent," a group of people to journey together through the Joshua 24 Experience.

You can define your tent in a number of different ways. Whether you choose your family, your small group, choose to start a new small group, invite a few neighbors, invite co-workers to meet together, join a new mid-size group at the church, form an online gathering, or connect with other students, the purpose is for all of us to experience Joshua 24 with others.

We encourage you to gather weekly with your tent. The following tent experience will help you dive deeper into each week's theme, spend time in the Word of God, support and pray for each other, and inspire you to live out each theme. We ask you to commit and participate with your tent for the next six weeks.

This guide is designed to follow the four main values of small group life at Eastview. We call them the "4G's." Each week you will journey through the 4G's in the following ways:

- **Gather** (your tent getting to know each other): Whether your tent has been together for years or you just met each other, this section will help each person "warm up" to the discussion and learn something new from each member along the way.

- **Grow** (your tent growing as Christ followers): One of the main goals for the Joshua 24 Experience is for everyone to grow in their walk with Jesus. This section helps your tent move through each week's scriptural and thematic content. *The goal is not to get through every question*, but to use the various parts to gain a deeper understanding of God and how Scripture is shaping our lives and experiences today. Use discretion as you work through this section.

  - **Your Covenant Story**: Each week you will be prompted to capture specific thoughts about your life that will culminate in an overview of your story and your journey with Jesus.

- **Give** (your tent serving each other): This section will provide you with a weekly spiritual discipline your tent can experience together. Each discipline is connected to the theme and provides a chance for your tent to put into practice the scriptural truths you learned in the Grow section. Be sure to provide enough time for your tent to go through this section.

- **Go** (your tent on mission): It's not enough to learn about each other, the Word, and to serve. We are also called to influence the world around us through the lives we live. This final section will provide easy ways for tent members to activate their Joshua 24 experience and impact their everyday community. Be sure to highlight this section and even refer back to it when you begin the next week's gathering.

If you choose to commit and participate, we are confident that you and your tent will have some amazing experiences over the next six weeks. In the words of Joshua 1:9, "Be strong and courageous. Do not be frightened, and do not be dismayed, for the LORD your God is with you wherever you go."

- Jason Sniff, on behalf of the entire Small Groups Team

REMEMBER

Gather

(your tent getting to know each other)

As you begin this week, take a few moments and allow each person to answer one of the following questions. If this is your first week together, be sure to introduce yourself and give some background information about yourself.

- What do you know about your family ancestry?
- Share a favorite family story or a story that has been passed down through your family.

Grow

(Your tent growing as Christ-followers)

- Read Joshua 24:1-13.
- **Watch and discuss the "Episode One: Remember" teaching video.**

- The Day 1 Daily Reading encouraged us to remember, reflect, and journal on God's work in our lives to this point. Share the parts of your story you wrote down. Go to the **Your Covenant Story** resource in the back of this book and complete the "Remember" section.

- In Joshua 24:7 God encourages Israel to remember that they've seen with their own eyes the work He did in Egypt. What have you personally seen God do in and through your life?

- In that same verse, God also acknowledges Israel's long wilderness journey. Many of us have experienced "wilderness" moments. These are times of difficulty, wandering without direction, or feeling uncomfortably distant from Jesus. Spend some time acknowledging your wilderness moments. How did you get through them?

- Joshua 24:8-12 highlights the hard-fought victories God provided for Israel. As you remember your story, share one or two victories God has won for you.

- As we look backwards in Israel's history, Genesis 12:1-3 records God's covenant promise of land, name, and nation to Abram (Abraham). How does Joshua 24:13 point to the fulfillment of this covenant promise? How has God fulfilled his promises in your life?

- Throughout Israel's history, they are called in various ways to remember the mighty works of God. Read Psalm 105:5-11 and Isaiah 44:21-23, and point out any "remembrance" language. What reminders do you have that prompt you toward giving thanks and worshipping the Lord?

- The early Church is also called to remember its story. Read Colossians 1:21-23 and take note of how Paul reminds the Colossians about that remembrance story.

  o you once were alienated and hostile in mind . . . (v. 21)

- o   he has now reconciled . . . (v. 22)
- o   you are holy and blameless . . . (v.22)

- Because of Jesus, we all have a remembrance story and are invited to share it with the world. Using Paul's words from Colossians 1, how would you finish the following phrases:

> o   I once was . . .
>
> _____
>
> _____
>
> o   Jesus has . . .
>
> _____
>
> _____
>
> o   I am now . . .
>
> _____
>
> _____

Give

(your tent serving each other)

- As Christ-followers, one of the most important ways we remember our Jesus story is by celebrating communion. Set aside some time in your gathering to read Luke 22:14-20 in remembrance of all that he has done and then participate in communion together. Let this lead you in to a time of prayer.

Go

(your tent on mission)

As you prepare to go and influence the world around you:

- Finish crafting your remembrance story and share it with someone this week.

- Write a note, send a text, or make a phone call and thank someone (family member, friend, spiritual mentor, small group member, boss, etc.) who has been influential in your life. Let them know specifically how they have helped you grow.

- Use the prayer exercise found in the Day 7 Daily Reading as a daily prayer guide for the next week.

- Continue reading the 40-day experience.

CHOOSE

Gather

(your tent getting to know each other)

We have a lot of choices to make on a daily basis. As you begin, choose one of the following questions to help everyone engage in conversation.

- Talk about the last major decision you made. What factors did you consider?
- Have you ever made a bad decision? How did you know it wasn't a good decision?

Grow

(your tent growing as Christ-followers)

- The Day 8 Daily Reading encouraged us to journal about our belief and our choice to follow Jesus. Share your answers to the following questions:
    - o Who do you believe Jesus to be?
    - o What is your choice about Him?

- o What is your, "as for me . . ." statement?
- Read Joshua 24:14-20 in two translations.
- **Watch and discuss the "Episode Two: Choose" teaching video**
- Our culture is full of counterfeit gods that vie for our attention and hearts. As a group, make a list of all the gods of our culture. Consider your group's list and answer the following:
  - o Which gods have enticed your family in the past?
  - o Which gods entice you personally?
- Joshua 24:16-20 records a crucial interaction between all the people of Israel and Joshua.
  - o What is their reply to his initial challenge?
  - o Why do you think Joshua responded the way he did in verses 19 and 20?
  - o What truth about God is Joshua trying to convey to the people of Israel and to us?
- In Joshua 23:6-8, the leaders of Israel are challenged to "cling" to the Lord. It is similar language to Genesis 2:24 and Matthew 19:5 that describe the oneness of a unified relationship between a married man and woman. What can we glean from these passages in light of our call to serve the Lord?
- Isaiah echoes the call for Israel to choose the god they will serve. Read Isaiah 45:20-25. What is clear about Isaiah's message? How have you seen this truth in your own life?
- Our choices are often the culmination of underlying thoughts and feelings. Their interactions are complicated but they move us toward or away from Jesus. Paul recognizes this and urges the Colossians church to seek and set their thoughts and feelings on Jesus above everything else. Read Colossians 3:1-4 and consider how your life choices move you toward or away from Jesus.

- Pastor Mike stated in the Day 8 Daily Reading, "Each of us individually has to choose the god (God) we are going to serve." If someone were to observe your life and daily actions from the last day, week, or month, what conclusions would they draw about whom you serve?

- Joshua warned the nation of Israel against choosing a duplicitous life, a life with one foot in the world and one foot with Jesus. He calls them to serve the Lord with sincerity and faithfulness. Sometimes, our temptation as Christ-followers is to soften our commitment to Jesus and to also follow some parts of this world. Take a few minutes and individually answer the questions posed from the Day 13 Daily Reading.

o   Is following Jesus worth all my relationships?
_____
_____

o   Is following Jesus worth all my possessions?
_____
_____

o   Is following Jesus worth all that I am?
_____
_____

Give

(your tent serving each other)

- We serve Him best within the context of other Christ-followers, and we thrive when we engage one another in the discipline of accountability. As you prepare to pray, find a way to break into groups of two or three and engage in the following spiritual formation:

- o Refer back to the list of counterfeit gods, and share the list of gods you need to dispose.
- o Submit yourself to being held accountable for the gods that entice you.
- o Pray over each other.
- o Choose to daily pray for each other until you gather together again.

GO

(your tent on mission)

- Finish crafting your "as for me and my house" statement. Write it out in the **Your Covenant Story** resource located in the back of the book. Consider adding simple phrases that clarify your statement. Using the phrase, "Others may . . . but I will choose . . ." will provide clarity. Examples can include:
  - o "Others may occasionally read the Bible, but I will choose to daily spend time in the Word."
  - o "Others may attend Sunday services sporadically, but I will choose to attend and engage weekly."
  - o "Others may hide their gods, but I will choose to hold myself accountable against the gods that tempt me."
- Share your Joshua 24 experience with someone around you. Let them know about your "as for me and my house" statement.
- Continue reading the 40-day experience.

REPENT

Gather

(your tent getting to know each other)

Choose one of the following questions to start the discussion for this week's experience.

- What was your most prized possession as a kid? Do you still have it today?

- Are you a person who quickly or slowly admits when you are wrong?

Grow

(your tent growing as Christ-followers)

- **Watch and discuss the "Episode Three: Repent" teaching video.**

- In the Day 15 Daily Reading Mike wrote about three idols many of us face. Take a few minutes and answer the following questions.

- o Relationships - Are there relationships in your life that are more important to you than God?
- o Materialism - Do you seek happiness and worth in the buying and accumulating of stuff?
- o Busyness – Does your current pace of life produce good fruit or exhaustion?
- Read Joshua 24:21-23 out loud. What key words jumped out as you heard this passage?
- The first action step Joshua calls Israel to do is to "put away the foreign gods that are among you." If Israel is going to be serious about their choice to follow God, they must directly deal with the sin in their life. Spend a few minutes reading the following passages either individually or as a group. Write down a few notes and discuss your answers with each other.

o   Joshua 23:11-13 - What warnings does Joshua give
     to the leaders of Israel?

     _____

     _____

o   Isaiah 30:18-22; Isaiah 44:9-22 - What does Isaiah
     say about idols and about the character of God?

     _____

     _____

o   Colossians 3:5-11 - Paul challenges the church of
     Colossae to put off a number of sins. Which sins
     on his list do you struggle with?

     _____

     _____

o   What are you called to put away?

     _____

     _____

- The second action step Joshua calls Israel to do is "incline
  your heart to the LORD." If we put away our sins, we are then
  called to fill our hearts with the things of God. Spend a few
  minutes reading the following passages either individually or
  as a group. Write down a few notes and discuss your answers
  with each other.

o   Joshua 22:5 - What does Joshua encourage the
    Eastern Tribes to do?

_____

_____

o   1 Kings 8:54-61 - What does King Solomon
    encourage all of Israel to do?

_____

_____

o   Colossians 3:12-17 - What does Paul encourage the
    church of Colossae to put on?

_____

_____

o   How are you called to incline your heart to the
    Lord?

_____

_____

- Take a few minutes and inventory the past week. What stole your time? Where did your resources and money go this week? What situations took your attention and focus away from Jesus? Do you notice any idols rearing their ugly heads?

- Repentance is a heart issue and requires some honesty. How did you answer the two questions posed in the Day 17 Daily Reading?

    o   Is my heart broken?
    o   Does my heart want to change?

Give

(your tent serving each other)

- We are being challenged this week to repent. One of the hardest things to do is confess our sins to another person, and yet the discipline of confession is healing and transforming. Confession inclines our hearts to the Lord. No matter how much shame or guilt we feel, as Christ-followers we have forgiveness. As you prepare to pray, break into your accountability groups and do the following:
    - o   Choose a person to read Psalm 32:1-7 aloud.
    - o   Take turns confessing and identifying one or two specific action steps.
    - o   After each person has shared, read Colossians 1:9-14 as a blessing and a reminder of our forgiveness through Jesus.
    - o   Complete the "Repent" section of the **Your Covenant Story** resources located in the back of the book.
    - o   Choose to daily pray for each other until you gather together again.

Go

(your tent on mission)

- Connect, call, or send a text of encouragement to your group members.

- Consider gathering your family and going through this week's family experience.

- Choose to fast from something this week in preparation for next week.

- Continue reading the 40-day experience.

WITNESS

Gather

(your tent getting to know each other)

We often find ourselves giving a good word for someone or something. Pick one of the following questions to kick start your discussion for this week.

- How do you remember important things? What reminders do you set in place?

- Talk about a time when you were called upon to be a witness or to give testimony about someone. What do you remember about it?

Grow

(your tent growing as Christ-followers)

- Take a few minutes and reflect on Sunday's service and dedication. What impacted you the most?

- Read Joshua 24:24-28 in two translations.

- **Watch and discuss the "Episode Four: Witness" teaching video.**
- The people of Israel gave testimony to whom they would follow and obey. Recall again the time when you chose to follow Jesus as your Lord and Savior.
    - o What was going on in your life at the time?
    - o What did you confess to Him and to others?
    - o What was it that convinced you to follow Him?
    - o If you are still deciding to follow Jesus, what intrigues you about becoming a Christ-follower?
- The covenant renewal between Israel and God has happened before. Take a look at Joshua 8:30-35. Joshua is obedient to the instructions Moses gave him in Deuteronomy 27:1-8.
    - o What similarities or differences do you see between these two covenant renewals?
    - o Take note of the people listed in the Joshua 8 passage. What does that list teach us about God's covenant?
    - o Recall any scripture that indicates who can be included in a covenant relationship with Jesus?
- Isaiah reminds Israel that God is a covenant-making and a covenant-keeping God. Read Isaiah 43:10-13 and Isaiah 46:8-11. What do these passages say about God and Israel?
- In his letter to the Colossians church, Paul gives witness to the preeminence of Jesus. As you read Colossians 1:15-20 aloud, emphasize all the "he" and "him" pronouns.
    - o What statements about Jesus resonate with you the most?
    - o Which statements can you give personal witness to?
- Paul encourages the Colossians to live out their witness. What specific instructions does he give them in Colossians 2:6-7? Which of those instructions are particularly helpful for you?
- Which of this week's Daily Readings impacts you the most?

- We are designed to follow Christ best within the context of other Christ followers. Read Hebrews 10:19-25. What covenant talk do you hear in this passage? Give witness to how your tent has helped you grow in your walk with Jesus.

- Joshua 24 is all about the covenant relationship between God and his people. Joshua deeply desires for Israel to fully live out this life-giving relationship with Yahweh. Take a moment and review the last four weeks.

> o **Week One: We were challenged to remember our history with Jesus.**
> o **Week Two: We were challenged to resolve once and for all whom we will follow, the world or Jesus.**
> o **Week Three: We were challenged to repent of any and all the things that keep us from fully following Jesus.**
> o **This week: We are being challenged to give witness to our covenant with Jesus.**

Jesus desires for His people to fully live out the deeply personal and communal alliance with Him and His people. Take time to complete the "Witness" portion of the **Your Covenant Story** resource.

Give

(your tent serving each other)

- As Christ-followers we have great opportunities to celebrate our covenant relationship with Jesus. The discipline of celebration is all about giving witness to the wonder-filled things he has done for us, in us, and through us. As a group, write out all the happenings (answered prayers, praises, wonders, miraculous situations, etc.) you have seen Jesus fulfill. Use this list to guide your prayer time.

Go

(your tent on mission)

- The word witness in Joshua 24 means "to tell what one has seen." As you prepare to influence the world around you this week, pray specifically for the following opportunities:
    - o Tell someone what you have seen Jesus do in your life.
    - o Ask your family (current or of origin) what they know to be true about Jesus.
    - o Decide upon a "covenant reminder" that will help you remember your commitment to the Lord. It could be a cross, a family seal, or a particular heirloom. Put this reminder in a prominent place in your home or workplace. Every time you see it, pause and celebrate the covenant relationship you have with Jesus.
- Continue reading the 40-day experience.

LEGACY

Gather

(your tent getting to know each other)

Use one of the following questions to start the discussion about spiritual legacy.

- Do you have a family heirloom that has been passed down through the generations? What makes that heirloom special?

- What do you remember most about your grandparents?

Grow

(your tent growing as Chris followers)

- Read Joshua 24:29-31. What initial thoughts do you have about this passage?

- **Watch and discuss the "Episode Five: Legacy" teaching video.**

- In Joshua's farewell speech to the leaders of Israel, what spiritual legacy does he highlight in Joshua 23:14? How do you see this legacy playing out in your life?

- The following passages are just a few of the many scriptures that point us toward experiencing an authentic relationship with Jesus. Read the following verses and write down what instructions they provide for covenant living that produces a spiritual legacy.

  ---

  o Isaiah 59:21 -

  _____

  _____

  o Colossians 1:28-29 -

  _____

  _____

  o Colossians 4:2-5 -

  _____

  _____

How will these insights lead us toward a lasting spiritual legacy?

What other verses come to mind that instruct us on covenant living?

- With encouragement toward covenant living, Scripture provides numerous warnings on covenant violations that can derail our legacy.

  o What warnings does Joshua give to the leaders of Israel in Joshua 23:15-16?
  o What warnings does Paul give the church of Colossae in Colossians 2:8-9,16-23?
  o How do these warnings apply to our lives today?

- Compare Judges 2:6-9 and Judges 2:10-15. What spiritual legacies are being lived out? Why is there such a stark difference between the generations? What dangers do we face as a church that might change our spiritual legacy?

- Psalm 145:4-7 reminds us of the importance of intergenerational living. In what ways do we see intergenerationality happening within our church?

- In the Day 29 Daily Reading, Mike encouraged us to think about our spiritual legacy and to write out what we want our legacy to be. Share with each other your writings and then take a few moments to record them in the "Legacy" section of the **Your Covenant Story** resource.

- A fearless church is best when all generations of Christ followers are represented and displaying ridiculous love and dangerous witness. Take a moment and review the Day 34 Daily Reading.

   o Who are your spiritual parents? Who are the brothers and sisters who push, influence, and love you?
   o How has the generation older than you influenced your spiritual legacy?
   o How are you influencing the generation younger than you?

Give

(your tent serving each other)

- Healthy spiritual legacies are created when Christ followers from across generations interact. It has been said that "life on life is God's greatest gift to us." The practice of discipleship guides us toward a mature relationship with God and His people. As you prepare to pray, break into your accountability groups and do the following:

- o Name one person who has intentionally helped you grow in your walk
  - o Pray over each other's spiritual legacy using Philippians 1:9-11 as a blessing.
- What are one or two ways your tent can serve other generations in the coming months?
- Take some time to figure out next steps with your tent. We encourage you to keep gathering after the Joshua 24 Experience is over.

Go

(your tent on mission)

- Commit one night this week and go through the family experience with your immediate family or your family of origin. You may choose to do it over a family meal, as part of a bedtime routine, or if distance is an issue, through an online chat forum.
- Start a discipleship relationship with a person older than you that you would like to learn from and/or one person younger than you that you would like to offer some guidance.
- Continue the 40-day experience.

REST

Gather

(your tent getting to know each other)

This week's study focuses on the rest that comes from a fulfilled covenant with God. Choose one of the following questions to help start the conversation. Allow time for each person to participate.

- What's the longest you've slept at one time? What's the longest you've gone without having sleep?

- Talk about a major project, task, or life situation that you persevered and saw to completion.

Grow

(your tent growing as Chris followers)

- Read Joshua 1:13, 11:23, 22:4, 23:1, and 24:32-33. What initial thoughts do you have about these passages?

- **Watch and discuss the "Episode Six: Rest" teaching video.**

197

- Some historians believe Israel lived in covenant rest for about seven years. This rest is described in Joshua 21:43-45 and is a continuation of Joshua 11:23. As you read these passages, discuss the following:
    - o What do these passages reveal about God?
    - o How do you envision this rest felt for the nation of Israel?
    - o In light of your current circumstances, what implications does this passage have for you?

- After many years of unrest and captivity, Isaiah reminds Israel of the covenant rest available through God. John writes of a similar rest for all who call themselves Christ-followers. Read and compare Isaiah 60:18-22 and Revelation 21:3-7. What appeals to you most about this kind of rest?

- There is another type of rest that comes from being Christ-followers. Spend some time talking about the identity and rest described in Isaiah 62:2-5 and Colossians 2:11-15.

- Joshua 24:32 describes the completion of God's covenant with Abraham from Genesis 12. Israel is now a great nation, has a name and covenant relationship with God, and now has land. In some ways this takes us back to the beginning of our tent experience. How have you seen God's covenant being fulfilled in your life?

- Paul encourages the Colossians to keep going in order to experience a fulfilled and mature life in Christ. What motivation do you receive from Colossians 1:28, 4:12, and 4:17?

- We were encouraged in the Day 36 Daily Reading to journal about the following questions. Take some time to share your answers with each other.
    - o What is your pattern of rest?

- o How can you practice the Sabbath?
- o What can you cut out of your schedule to create needed space?

- Most of us live full or over-full lives anticipating that our activities will bring us satisfaction. Often, however, our full lives leave us exhausted and unfulfilled. Why is that? What parts of your busy life do not bring fulfillment? What are you willing to do about it?

- Rest provides us invaluable time with God, ourselves, and others. How do you want rest to be a part of your story? Mike referenced three ways to practice rest by diverting daily, withdrawing weekly, and retreating regularly. Complete the last section of the **Your Covenant Story** entitled "Rest." Then, take some time to share your completed covenant story.

Give

(your tent serving each other)

- The disciplines of silence and solitude are crucially important to the health and longevity of our lives. Creating space to sit gives our minds and hearts space to hear what our Lord has been trying to tell us. As a group, take 5-10 minutes and practice silence. Find a comfortable spot and turn off all distractions. Just sit and breathe. How might this practice be an ongoing help for you?

- Choose to stay as one or break into your smaller accountability groups for prayer time. Take a few moments to confess what you need rest from and then pray together. Have someone close your prayer time by reading Philippians 1:3-11 aloud.

Go

(your tent on mission)

- The discipline of first and last is a practice where you set aside the first and last minutes of each day to spend with Jesus. For the next seven days, determine the time you will set aside and put this discipline into practice.

- Determine next steps for your tent. Will you continue to gather? Do some in your tent need to reconnect in a small group? Commit to helping each person find his or her next step.

YOUR COVENANT STORY

Remember – I remember what Jesus has done in and through my life:

_____

_____

_____

Choose – As for me and my house I choose:

_____

_____

_____

Repent – I will put away the following idols/sin that keep me from fully following Jesus:

_____

_____

_____

Witness – I know this to be true of Jesus:

_____

_____

_____

Legacy – I will leave the following spiritual legacy:

_____

_____

_____

Rest – I will establish the following rhythms of rest:
Divert daily

_____

_____

_____

Withdraw weekly

_____

_____

_____

Retreat regularly

_____

_____

_____

HOW TO USE THE FAMILY EXPERIENCE

You might choose to do this as your only tent experience, or you might do the family experience in addition to your small group. Each week we've given you more than you can use so that you can pick and choose activities or discussions based on the personality of your family and the age of your kids.

Opening Activities

You'll start with a couple of options for an opening game or discussion based on the age of your kids. If you have kids all up and down the age spectrum, mix it up a little so that you keep everyone engaged.

Teaching Time

Next you'll read the biblical text for the week. Choose a translation that is easy to understand for the youngest person in the family. Then watch the video Mike's video. If your kids don't know who Mike is, introduce him. The videos are short and move right along, but if you have little ones, they could always color their Joshua 24 Experience coloring page for the day while you watch it.

Family Discussion

There you will find several options for discussion. You won't have time to do them all. As a matter of fact, a good rule of thumb is to keep things moving and not land on anything longer than the age of your kids. So, a 7 year old might need you to switch things up in seven minutes or less.

Family Activities

Finally, you will find some additional activities with creative ideas for making memories and taking the Joshua 24 Experience a little further.

Don't worry if week one doesn't go quite as you hope. Be patient and stay at it. Being the spiritual leader in your family is the most important thing you can do for them, but it's a marathon, not a sprint. If this type of thing is new to your family, learn to make faith conversations at home a healthy part of your family's rhythm. Use this Joshua 24 Experience as a launching point to create a wonderful atmosphere of grace and faith in your home where your children grow in the grace and knowledge of Jesus under your leadership.

Family Experience
WEEK ONE - REMEMBER

Joshua 24:2-3

Theme Builder Activities

To help get your kids engaged in today's discussion, start out with one of these ideas that have to do with remembering. If you have a mix of the age groups, do a little of each.

- For PreK through 5th grade: Play a memory/matching game – digital versions are available for free in the App Store and Google Play or online at Sprout or PBS Kids. Matching card games are available in toy sections and come in all types of themes.

- For JH & HS Students: Tell funny stories of when the kids were little. Break out old videos or pictures and have fun talking about some favorite family memories.

Transition: "It's good for us to take time to remember special things from our past. Today we are going to see how God called the Israelites to remember his faithfulness to them."

Teaching

- Read Joshua 24:2-3 together. Pick a version the youngest person in the family can understand.

- Watch Mike's Teaching Video. If the kids don't know Mike, explain who he is.

Discussion

Based on the ages of your kids, choose from the discussion topics below to foster a good faith conversation with your children.

- Discuss the teaching video. What did you learn? What challenged you? What encouraged you? Can you think of any time when you might have missed seeing God moving in your life only to recognize it clearly later.

- Tell your kids your personal faith story. When did you begin to put your faith in Jesus? Talk about the points from the daily reading on Day Five. If you share about a time in your life when you were not following God; based on the ages of your kids, use discretion on the details of your sinful choices.

- Talk to your kids about your family's spiritual family tree. Are you the first person in your family to follow Jesus or do you come from a lineage of Christians?

- In Joshua 24 God reminds the Israelites that they saw with their own eyes that He brought them out of Egypt and through the wilderness. It is important to take the time to remember God's faithfulness in the past. Share stories with your kids about how God has helped you personally or as a family.

- Ask your kids if they have any stories of their own about how God has helped them in the past.

- Referring to the daily reading from Day 2, ask your kids if they have ever felt like God has forgotten them.

- With your older kids, referring to Day 2, have a discussion about whether or not they feel like God has forgotten the world. Where does He seem to be missing?

Life Application

- We've shared stories tonight about how God has been faithful to our family. He has helped us through sticky situations and tough times. We can trust that God is going to be faithful in the future, even if we sometimes can't see it until a situation has passed.

- God remembers us – he sees us and knows us. We can trust that God will keep his promises in our lives like he did in Israel's. He promises to forgive our sins, to help us grow, to use us in this world to do his good work, and to take us home to be with him in heaven forever.

Family Activities

- Pick-A-Prayer Jar – Taking your cue from Day 7, create a jar with slips of paper that have different names/topics written on them. Include names of families and friends, missionaries, leaders, etc., and each night at bedtime or dinner, have one family member draw a slip of paper and pray for that person or topic. You could even have every family member draw a slip and pray.

- A Family Sabbath Plan – Referring to Day 3, discuss having a family Sabbath. What would it look like to have a time when no one worked, did chores or homework, and everyone spent a block of time resting, recreating and replenishing both together and separately? When would you have it? What would it look like? What if something comes up that conflicts with it? Avoid legalism and remember the Sabbath by remembering the heart of it – rest. Check out the book <u>24/6</u> by Matthew Sleeth, MD for some inspiration and practical ways of pulling this off. You may decide that this better fits the final week of the study, even though we cover it in our reading on Day Three.

- Take Communion As A Family – Referring to the daily reading on Day 6, close out your time together today by taking communion, remembering Jesus' body and blood and the forgiveness we have through him. Any type of bread or drink will do, so pull out the Goldfish crackers and Grape Kool-Aid and make a memory.

- A Spiritual Scrapbook – create a journal or a scrapbook where you collect stories/pictures from your family members showing when God has been faithful to your family.

Family Guide
WEEK TWO - CHOOSE
Joshua 24:14-21

Theme Builder Activities

To help get your kids engaged in today's discussion, start out with one of these ideas that have to do with choosing. If you have a mix of the age groups, do a little of each.

- For PreK through 8th grade: Play a quick game of "Would you Rather..." A quick search online will provide you with some creative questions if you need some ideas. Go around the room asking each person to answer the same question or give each person a new one. An example is "Would you rather be able to run at 100 mph or fly at 10 mph?" You can get heavier with the questions like "Would you rather continue with your life or start your life over?"

- HS Students: Talk about big choices that your teenager is working through right now or will be in the near future: class choices, dating, getting a job, trying out for something, choosing a college, etc.

Younger Option Transition: "Now these are kind of fun, but we really will never have to choose between running 100 mph or flying at 10 mph. But today, we are going to talk about a choice that we really do need to make in life."

Older Option Transition: "These are all important choices and some of them have a big impact on your future. That's all the more reason that today's conversation is really important. The decision we make about today's topic is the most important decision we'll make and it affects all of these other choices we just talked about."

Teaching

- Read Joshua 24:14-21 together. Pick a version the youngest person in the family can understand.

- Watch Mike's Teaching Video.

Discussion

Based on the age of your kids, choose from the discussion topics below to foster a good faith conversation with your children.

- Discuss today's teaching video. What did they learn? What challenged them the most? What questions do they have about the video?

- Why do you think Joshua told the Israelites to pick what seemed best to them, even though he really wanted them to choose to serve God? (verse 15)

- Why do you think he told them "no" after they said they wanted to serve him? (verses 19-20)

- On Day 8 of the daily readings, you wrote down a confession of your faith and your decision to follow Jesus – talk to your kids about your choice. Maybe share what you wrote down. Ask them what they believe about Jesus.

- Even though we are talking about choosing God this week, refer to Day 9 of your daily reading and talk to your kids about how it makes them feel to know that God has chosen them.

- Referring to the daily reading from Day 10, ask your family to name some other things that the world around us chooses instead of God. Make that more personal and ask if there are things that draw our attention away from God. Even if we have made the big decision to choose God, each day presents an opportunity to choose whether or not we will walk in His ways. Encourage each other to choose God daily, but also emphasize the grace and mercy of God when we do choose poorly. (1 John 1:9)

- One of the big choices we all make is in choosing our friends. Referring to Day 11, talk about how important it is to choose good friends. While it is good to have friends from all walks of life, our closest friends (girlfriends and boyfriends included) should share our values. (1 Corinthians 15:33 and Proverbs 13:20)

- Referring to Day 13, discuss how being a Jesus follower is not always easy. Ask them about the challenges they face being a Christian. Ask them what they feel like they've had to give up because they are a Christian.

- Look up Robert Frost's "The Road Not Taken" online and read it as a family. Read Matthew 7:13-14 and John 14:6 (referenced in Mike's video) and discuss what it means to choose the path less chosen or the narrow path.

Life Application Talking Points:

- In this week's verses, Joshua created a fork in the road experience for the Israelites. Today, your family is looking at that same fork in the road. We have a choice to make in our own lives. Have a moment of commitment where as a family you embrace Joshua 24:15 "...But as for me and my house, we will serve the Lord."

211

- Talk to your kids about how making that choice impacts every other choice we make in life. When we follow God and walk in his ways, we know that He will lead us on the best path – though not always the easiest.

Optional Family Activities:

- **Dedication Moment** – When your family discusses Joshua 24:15 "...but as for me and my house, we will serve the Lord," take a moment to pray as a family and place a marker in your home of that moment. It will go along with a dedication service we will have in two weeks at Eastview. Consider purchasing (available in places like Hobby Lobby) or making some wall art featuring Joshua 24:15 and put it in a prominent place in your home.

- **Baptism Discussion** – This coming Sunday is a "Baptism Sunday" at Eastview during the services. If you or your children have not yet taken that step in your faith, consider having a conversation about that this week. If you have elementary aged kids, watch this video together at https://www.youtube.com/watch?v=n0kzf9fHcKY.

- **Identity In Christ Video** – To take the discussion about being chosen by God a little further, watch the animated video "Your Identity in Christ" to affirm your kids. Particularly great for older elementary kids through adults, this sketchpad animation will help your family realize the worth you receive by being chosen and having an identity in Christ. https://www.youtube.com/watch?v=hsDQEb-qlyM (1:38)

- **Family Piggy Bank** – Whether you choose a piggy bank or a treasure chest or a mason jar, choose something you would normally put money in, and over the years fill it with slips of paper with stories of times your family "stored up treasures in heaven" by giving financially to God's good work in this world. Perhaps it's a story of when your child emptied their bank for Imagine, or when you started tithing, or you gave to the Christmas offering and helped free slave children in India, or paid for someone's groceries, or began supporting a missionary.

- **Serving Suggestion** – Referring to Day 14 of the Daily Reading, check out these ideas below on ways that your family can serve together:

  o **OUTSIDE THE HOME:** Make memories this year by serving outside of the home as a family. These can be fun occasions and teach valuable lessons.

    ▪ Rake an elderly person's yard together (don't take $!).
    ▪ Leave secret gifts for a needy family on their porch, knock on the door and run!
    ▪ Volunteer at a 5k or charity event together.
    ▪ Host an international student for dinner.
    ▪ Babysit for an adoptive family.
    ▪ Secretly wash a neighbor's car early in the morning and then go get donuts.
    ▪ Pass out smiles and flowers at a nursing home.
    ▪ Make dinner for a family with a newborn.
    ▪ Send care packages to soldiers or college students.

  o **SERVING AT EASTVIEW**

    ▪ **Seize the Moments at Eastview** Whether it's our quarterly food drives, Imagine, cleaning days, etc., use the various all-church initiatives as opportunities to engage your children. As you take them to help you do the shopping for the Food Pantry, for example, you are building memories and important lessons in their hearts.
    ▪ **Pitching In** Look for opportunities as a family to pitch in when you can with informal

213

opportunities for serving. For example, after a church function, stick around and help clean up and put things away. After Sunday service, go through the hallways and pick up trash. Show up on a Saturday for an hour and help clean up litter or weeds. Help the kids to see the church as "our church." Help them develop ownership and to build a mindset of being a servant.

- **Family Missions Trip** There are options available for families to take an international missions trip. For more information, stop by the Missions kiosk on the upper level or check out upcoming trips at www.eastview.church/outreach/global.
- **The Food Pantry** Working in Eastview's Food Pantry is a great opportunity for families to serve together.
- **Serving Opportunities For Your Child** There are places your child can serve on his or her own at Eastview. Junior High and High School students can help in the Eastview Kids programs, the Student Ministry Programs, Building Services, Food Pantry, Café 19 and more! Elementary kids can serve on an arts team like drama, choir, sound and lights or art. Each grade level has opportunities to serve in its own area on Sundays. Some opportunities are for the service the child usually attends, and others are for times when the child is not usually in the service. Selecting a time when the child is not normally in a service works well if you are serving one service/attending the other service, too. Talk to your child's pastor to get more information.

Family Guide
WEEK THREE - REPENT
Joshua 24:23&24

Theme Builder Activities

To help get your kids engaged in today's discussion, start out with one of these ideas that have to do with repenting. If you have a mix of the age groups, do a little of each.

- For PreK through Early Elementary: Play a game of "What Time Is It Mr. Fox?" which acts out the idea of turning away and turning towards (repenting).

- For 8 year olds through High School: Secret Leader can be a fun game for your family, especially if you have a large family. Family members will sit in a circle with one person who is "it." A secret leader will have the family changing actions while the person who is "it" is trying to figure out who that leader is. No need to prep and you can play for as long or as short a period of time as you like. For full game rules, check http://www.group-games.com/ and search for *Follow The Leader,* or go to http://www.group-games.com/action-games/follow-the-leader.html.

Transition for younger option: "When we repent from our sins, it's kind of like this game – we're heading the wrong way towards sin and we need to turn from it and change our ways."

Transition for older option: "When we repent from our sins, we have to do more than just feel badly about our sin. We need to change our behavior as well."

Teaching

- Read Joshua 24:21-24 together. Pick a version the youngest person in the family can understand.
- Watch Mike's Teaching Video.

Discussion

Based on the ages of your kids, choose from the discussion topics below to foster a good faith conversation with your children.

- Discuss today's video. What did you think of as Mike was talking? When Mike talked about how we are not really as lost as we think we might be, how did that make you feel? When Mike said we need to get good at repenting, what does it look like to repent every day?

- In verse 23, Joshua commands the people to throw away their foreign gods and to give themselves completely to God. Discuss as a family the things that keep us from giving ourselves completely to God.

- In the daily reading on Day 15 you wrote down the idols in your life. If appropriate, share some of these with your family, in particular any of them that have caused your family pain. Make sure that they know it is safe to be honest in your home and emphasize the grace that is ours through Jesus.

- Using the 3 steps in the Daily Reading on Day 16, teach your kids what it means to repent. (This would be a great time to use the Fire Pit idea below in the Optional Family Activities.)
  - o Tell God He's right.
  - o Tell God you're wrong.
  - o Tell him you want to "throw away" your sins.

- Referring to the reading on Day 18, talk as a family about how stopping sinful behavior or habits is hard. Repenting means to change your mind, and that means that you not only turn away from sin, but turn towards God. How can turning to God help you overcome the temptation to continue to stay in your sin? What does it look like to turn to God?

- Read Matthew 18:21-22 and talk about how Jesus painted a picture of ridiculous forgiveness. First of all, he told Peter that he should never stop forgiving. Talk about how Jesus would not command us to do something he would not do. Talk about how the servant in the parable owed more money than he could ever pay back, and how that is a picture of our sin. Read 1 John 1:9. Consider using the *Optional Family Activity: Quiet Time* as a follow up to this conversation.

Life Application

- God wants us to be completely His. He wants us to get rid of the things that keep us from that (Hebrews 12:1). As a family, we can help each other by praying for each other (Hebrews 13:18), calling each other out when we see things that others might be blind to (Colossians 3:16), and forgiving each other as God has forgiven us (Ephesians 4:32).

- Repentance is something we should do every day. We need to confess our sins to God and ask his forgiveness, and he promises to forgive us (1st John 1:9).

Family Activities:

- Fire Pit – Have a fire in the fire pit and give each person a piece of paper. Give them time to think and pray on their own. Have them write down a sin (or a list of sins) on their paper and encourage them to repent of that sin. When they are ready, have them throw their paper in the fire as they ask God to forgive them of their sins. You can read out loud as a family or have each person read on their own verses like Psalm 103:8-13 (God removes our sin as far as the east is from the west); 1 John 1:9 (God is faithful and just and will forgive us our sins); Isaiah 43:25 (remembers your sins no more); Micah 7:18-19 (delights in mercy – hurled our sins to the bottom of the sea); Colossians 1:13-14 (rescued us – we have the redemption and forgiveness of sins). Wrap up saying, "Just like we cannot reach into the fire and pull our papers back out, God cannot bring your sin back on you. He chooses to forget – to not hold that against you anymore – and that's a promise. Only the devil will try to continue to accuse you of that sin, but God has taken it away and we are no longer guilty of it. That's forgiveness."

- Quiet Time (Older kids) – We have included below some lists of sins that Paul includes in his letters. After your discussion time, give everyone time and space to reflect on today's topic by going through a list or two (or all of them). Have each person ask God to reveal his or her sin as they think through the list. Encourage them to spend time praying and repenting, asking God for his forgiveness and the strength to change.

   o   Romans 1:26-31
   o   1 Corinthians 6:9-10
   o   Galatians 5:19-21
   o   Ephesians 4:25-31
   o   Colossians 3:5-7
   o   2 Timothy 3:1-7

Family Guide
WEEK FOUR - WITNESS

Joshua 24:26&27

Theme Builder Activities

To help get your kids engaged in today's discussion, start out with one of these ideas that have to do with keeping or marking a commitment. If you have a mix of the age groups, do a little of each.

- For Families with all ages: Play the card game "I Doubt It" (known also by other non-family-friendly names). The name of the game is saying something you don't mean without getting caught. For family friendly instructions on how to play, check out grandparents.com. After playing, talk about how today you are going to look at saying what you mean to God and keeping your promise.

- For Families with all ages: Discussion about keeping promises: Can you remember ever breaking a promise? What is a funny promise that you made to someone? Is it ever okay to break a promise? What are some ways people seal a promise (just say it, pinky swear, spit in your hand and shake, wedding vows/rings, etc.)?

- For Families with all ages: Have a good old-fashioned trust fall. Have your child stand with his or her back to you and have them fall back into your arms. Assure them that you will catch them and see if they can fall without reservation. You can up the thrill factor for your older kids by doing a "group catch" as your child falls from a bench. You should search for a video online of this version if you haven't seen it before so that you can do this safely. Talk about how they expected you to keep your word to catch them, and how it's important to keep your promises.

Transition: In our discussion today we are going to see where the Israelites made a promise to God to change their lives – that's a big promise. And to remember that promise, they set up a special rock.

Teaching

- Read Joshua 24:25-27 together. Pick a version the youngest person in the family can understand.

- Watch Mike's Teaching Video.

Discussion

Based on the age of your kids, choose from the discussion topics below to foster a good faith conversation with your children.

- Talk about the video by asking questions like: What did they learn? What questions do they have? What stood out to them? What inspired them? What challenged them?

- Make sure that your family understands what a covenant. Mike said that it is an agreement, or a promise, between two people.

- Referring to Day 22 in the daily reading, talk about Eastview's vision statement as a family.

- o A fearless church of Christ followers who ridiculous love and dangerous witness are irresistible.
- o Ask them what they think a fearless church is like.
- o Talk about what ridiculous love is and how you can show it as a family.
- o Discuss what they think of when they hear the term "dangerous witness."
- o Ask what it means for Eastview, and your family in particular, to be irresistible to those around you who don't follow Jesus.

- Mike ended today's video challenging us to bear witness to each other. Use one of the optional dedication ideas below in the Family Activities, or simply have a discussion asking each person in the family to share what his or her commitment to Jesus is.

- Read Ecclesiastes 5:1-7 and talk about how making a commitment this week is very serious to God. While he gives us his forgiveness when we mess up, he also wants us to take our decision to follow him very seriously. (Refer to Counting the Costs discussion from Week 2.)

- Referring to Day 25 in the Daily Reading, ask your kids if they, like Israel, have ever wondered if "God has stopped loving them." What makes them feel that way? What can we do if we ever start to wonder that? Read Romans 8:38-39 together to remind them that nothing can separate us from the love God.

- In the daily reading for Day 27, you wrote about your good fight. Share what you wrote with your family and ask them how they see their life as the "good fight." Check out the optional family activity below on the persecuted church to take this discussion further.

- Discuss the idea of our life being a race as described in Daily Reading Day 28. Talk about the cloud of witnesses. Talk about how the arena is full, we have a race to win and Jesus is at the finish line rooting us on. See the family activities below for an idea to take this to the next level.

Life Application

- This week, we as a family, are making a commitment (to follow God or be a part of what God is doing here at Eastview) and are going to mark that commitment by dedicating a special Celebration Rock at church this Sunday. This means that we are saying that our family is going to be all about following God in this life.

- We can make that decision as a family, but it's also important for you to make your own decision to follow Jesus.

Family Activities

- **Witness Rock Visit** – After the Witness Rock Celebration concludes this Sunday, or sometime during the following week, plan a visit with your family to have a personal time together. Take time to pray and make a specific family commitment. You can use Mike's suggestion from the video and use verse 24 as your family's prayer: "We will serve Jesus our God and obey him." Take a picture of your family in front of the rock and plan to return each year to renew your commitment and take another picture. Over the years, you can have a collection of photos to remind you of your family's commitment to being about God's good work in this world.

- **Family Witness Rock** – At your home, set up a witness rock of your own to serve as a reminder of the commitment your family is making this week. It could be a pile of rocks as in Joshua 4 or one large rock as in Joshua 24. It could be a garden stone that you make from a kit (available at a hobby or art store) and carve into it a message and your names. Date it and have a simple dedication service where you make the Joshua 24:24 commitment Mike discussed in today's video: "We will serve Jesus our God and obey him."

Pray and Support the Persecuted Church – Referring to Day 27 of your Daily Reading, talk about the fact that throughout the world there are many people who follow Jesus though it is very dangerous. More people die for their faith today than at any other point in history. Visit the websites of Voice of the Martyrs (www. persecution.com) or Open Doors (www.opendoorsusa.org) to find resources to help your family learn about, pray for and support persecuted Christians around the world.

Watch a Race – Take your family to a race (HS track meet, marathon or a local 5K but a large crowd will make a bigger point) along with this book and talk to your kids about the points made in the daily reading for Day 28. Talk about how the crowd is like the cloud of witnesses. Discuss how hard the runners are working to run their race and how that is like life. Talk about how Jesus is waiting for us at the finish line. If you can't make it to a race, you could substitute the race for a movie like McFarland USA or Cars.

Family Guide
WEEK FIVE - LEGACY

Joshua 24:29-31

Theme Builder Activities

To help get your kids engaged in today's discussion, start out with one of these ideas that have to do with legacy. If you have a mix of the age groups, do a little of each.

- For Families with all ages: Get out pictures of you when you were a child. Look at pictures through the years of both you and the kids and look for similarities in each other. Talk about the ways your kids take after you. How do you look the same? How do you act the same? What interests do you share? And so on…

- For Families with all ages: In today's video, Mike finds evidence that others have already been out to a remote part of the desert before he arrives and connects that to those who've gone before us in life. Ask the kids if they have ever thought about the fact that at one point, you were *their* age. Talk about what it was like for you… what you did, what school was like, what you were afraid of, what pressures you faced, etc.

Transition: Today we are going to discuss leaving a legacy of faith for those who are coming after us. A legacy is something that is passed down to you from your parents, or something you pass on to your children. You can also leave a legacy by making a difference that lasts beyond your time.

Teaching

- Read Joshua 24:29-31 together. Pick a version the youngest person in the family can understand.
- Watch Mike's Teaching Video.

Discussion

Based on the age of your kids, choose from the discussion topics below to foster a good faith conversation with your children.

- Talk about the video by asking questions like: What did they learn? What questions do they have? What stood out to them? What inspired them? What challenged them?

- In today's video, Mike talked about how Moses left Joshua a legacy of being a SERVANT of the Lord. Have a discussion on what has been passed down to you from your parents. Ask the kids if there are things they are learning from you (risky, I know!) Maybe you have things that were passed on to you that were not healthy and you can discuss how you are trying to change that for your kids.

- On Day 29 you spent time thinking about your legacy. If there are things that you need to communicate to your spouse or children, take time to discuss the legacy you want to leave them.

- Ask your kids how they can leave a legacy even while they are young. You might have to help them see how they can

225

make a difference that lasts beyond them. For example, your high schooler can talk about making an impact on the underclassmen so that when they graduate, the ones coming behind them will benefit from their influence. Even young kids have opportunities to impact younger siblings, or other kids at church and school.

- Read Judges 2:10 – "After that whole generation [died], another generation grew up who knew neither the Lord nor what he had done for Israel." Ask your kids what they think happened. How did a whole generation grow up who didn't know God and all the amazing things he had done for them? Could that happen today? What can we do about it?

- Referring to Day 30 in the Daily Readings, we cannot assume our kids understand our faith. One way to lead your family spiritually is to be a safe person they can ask their questions about our faith. Have a Q&A time with your kids and see if there is anything they don't understand, have a hard time believing or questions about certain topics. Never be afraid to say, "that's a great question, but I'm not sure how to answer that. Let me look into and we'll talk about it some more later." And then don't forget to follow up.

- Use the reading from Day 32 to form a discussion about Ephesians 6:1-4. If the kids are not reading this book, consider having them read the section entitled "Children/Students." Risk asking your kids if there is anything you've done to "provoke them to anger" or if you have hurt them in any way. Make this a healing time. Ask the kids what it looks like to obey and honor their parents. Discuss what it's like when they disobey or dishonor you. Make sure this discussion is full of truth, love and grace.

- Referring to Day 33 of the daily reading, have a discussion about how your kids can set an example in speech, conduct, love, faith and purity. Talk about how they can set an example at church, at home, at school or at their job.

- In Day 34 of the daily reading we covered the "family" we have in the church. Talk to your kids about the "church family" and ask them who fits the roles described in Day 34. Bring in the idea from Day 35 that we have a long "family history" in the church.

Life Application

- We've seen how Joshua left a legacy of faith so that the nation of Israel was dedicated to God even after he died. We have an opportunity to help the people who are younger than us know Jesus and what he has done for us. We can encourage and inspire those coming behind us to follow Jesus and do his good work in this world.

- God has given us the responsibility to raise you to know him and show you how to live for him. He has given you the command to honor and obey us. That should impact our behavior, attitudes and relationships in a positive way.

Family Activities

- **Family Culture** - As you talk about legacy, think about the environment you want your child to be raised in. Maybe you want it to be much like the home you grew up in, or maybe you don't want it looking anything like that! Take some time to determine what your family culture is going to be. Family culture pieces are a popular item in home décor right now. They are often titled something like: "In our family, we do..." followed by a list of attributes and activities like forgiveness, hugs, laughter, football, patience, dinners together, etc. Prayerfully determine a family culture that you would like to establish in your home, and dedicate your home and family to God. There are many family culture pieces that are already made and can be purchased online or at a home décor store. They range from small plaques to large vinyl wall decals. You might consider creating your own, adding some faith elements that might not appear on other ones. There are even sites where you can customize/personalize Christian wall art like www.littlelifedesigns.com. Whether you decide to make your own or buy one, make sure that your family culture is visible as a reminder of the expectations of how your family will live. These would be the things you would want your kids to recall when they're out on their own or you're no longer together.

- **Letters From Parents To Your Family** – Take time to write letters to each of your family members, spouse included, about what you want for them in life. Include any apologies that you need to give. Plan some time alone with each person. Go get a cup of coffee, chips and salsa or some ice cream and read your letter to them. Then give them the letter and pray a special blessing over their life.

- **Doorpost Scriptures** - In the Daily Reading on Day 30, Mike references the practice of Jewish families to place scrolls of scripture on the door posts of the house (Deuteronomy 6:4-6). Take that concept and create a place in your home where your family can display scripture verses. You can leave a verse on your kids' bathroom mirrors. Create a graffiti wall in your home where everyone can add verses to the wall. Or choose a family verse like Joshua 24:15 "As for me and my house we will serve the Lord" or a family blessing like Zephaniah 3:17 "The Lord your God is with you, he is mighty to save. He takes great delight in you. He will quiet you with his love. He will rejoice over you with singing." Then create a way to display it in your home. Paint it on a wall, or create a cool chalkboard design or even purchase a piece of art with the verse on it.

- **Connect with the Older Generation** – In Day 31 in the daily reading, we see how both you and your kids need time to listen to the older generation. Create space for these conversations by getting together with your parents. Or if they are not accessible, consider seeking out an older neighbor or someone from the church who can speak into your life and the lives of your children as only someone who has lived longer can. Invite them over for a cookout or offer to bring over dessert. Many children don't get quality time with their grandparents, so do what you can to make that connection for them.

Family Guide
WEEK SIX - REST

Joshua 24:32

Theme Builder Activities

To help get your kids engaged in today's discussion, start out with one of these ideas that have to do with rest.

- For PreK through 5th grade (older ones too if they're game): We've been using the term "tent" for this study. For fun, put up a tent in the family room made of bed sheets and clothes pins, pull out the sleeping bags, get out the flashlights, get everyone in their PJs and have a campout in the living room tonight while you go through today's discussion. You could also set a tent up outside and make it a back yard camp out, which will go nicely with today's teaching. You can also just skip a tent all together and just "camp out" in the family room to reinforce today's theme of REST.

- For JH & HS Students: Create a totally chill evening. Declare a night with no chores (and no homework if you can manage it), and just spend the night relaxing and having fun. If your budget allows, have carryout or delivery for dinner, or something simple from the freezer so that *you* don't have to do a lot of work either.

Transition: Tonight we're just taking it easy and getting some extra rest. God actually has a lot to say about rest and how important it is.

Teaching

- Read Joshua 24:32 together. Pick a version the youngest person in the family can understand.

- Watch Mike's Teaching Video.

Discussion

Based on the age of your kids, choose from the discussion topics below to foster a good faith conversation with your children.

- Talk about the video by asking questions like: What did they learn? What questions do they have? What stood out to them? What inspired them? What challenged them?

- Read Exodus 20:8-10. Explain what the Sabbath was. Discuss why you think God made this one of the "big 10" and why this is the longest commandment? Discuss what it would look like in your family to create a "Sabbath-like" rest in your weekly rhythm.

- If you had that discussion about a family Sabbath during week one, do a check-up. How have you done keeping a Sabbath rest in your family's weekly rhythm? What is working? What is tripping you up? What is confusing about having a Sabbath?

- Discuss these paragraphs from Mike's writing on Day 37:

> *"God is telling us that a seven-day work week is not more productive than working six days. If you want a productive work life, if you want to accomplish a lot in life, if you want to get that project done, if you want to graduate from college, a weekly rest day is the way to go. I've led staff*

members before with this line: "You may be exceptional, but you're not the exception. If God takes a rest day, then so should you. He is just as pleased when you rest in him as when you work for him."

"Though most of us aren't farmers any more, the Sabbath still applies, no matter how busy the season is. These days we are tempted to skip rest to study for finals, to prepare for the annual report, or to clean the house for the holidays. We work seven days in a row to finish the school project. We say yes to "over time" in order to make more money during the holidays. We take second jobs to send our kids to college. Never separated from our jobs, we manage to work on our "day off" to clear all the emails from our iPhones. We talk about, "when things slow down" but continue to pack our calendars with social events, work meetings, kids' events, and travel. God says, "stop, cease, pause, sabbath". We're exhausted as a result. We have convinced ourselves that we can live 24/7 lives when God specifically designed us for 18/6 ones."

- Mike quoted another teacher who told him to "divert daily," "withdraw weekly" and "retreat regularly." Discuss as a family what this might look like in your home.

- The practice of Sabbath gave the Jewish people time to let their bodies and minds rest. It gave space for worship and time together. What kind of things could you do as individuals and as a family on a "Sabbath" day? (Go for picnics, plays games, read books, have a family devotion, have a movie night, eat leftovers or order in, etc.)

- Referring to Day 38 in our Daily Reading, talk to your kids about being emotionally and spiritually exhausted by trying to live up to everyone's expectations. Give yourselves space to talk about the expectations you all have from each other, yourselves, church, teachers, friends, social media, etc. Read Matthew 11:28-30 together and talk about what it looks like to "come" to Jesus so that he can give us rest.

- In the final day of reading, Mike concludes reflecting on the fact that our faith leads ultimately to rest – an eternal Sabbath rest. Discuss as a family how you can live now in light of the fact that the Bible refers to eternal life as eternal rest.

Life Application

- God wants us to rest. He designed us to rest. He commands it. When we do a good job resting the right amount of time – not too much and not too little, we live the healthiest type of life – the type of life that God wants for us.

Family Activities

- **A Family Sabbath Plan** – (Repeat option from Week One). Discuss having a family Sabbath. What would it look like to have a time where no one worked, did chores or homework and everyone spent a block of time resting, recreating and replenishing themselves together and separately? When would you have it? What would it look like? What if something comes up that conflicts with it? If there are work schedules of parents or older kids that have work schedules that prevent one full day for the family, how could you get creative with this idea? Avoid legalism and remember the Sabbath by remembering the heart of it – rest. Check out the book 24/6 by Matthew Sleeth, MD for some inspiration and practical ways of pulling this off.

- **A Family Retreat** – Either by creating a new experience or just tweaking something you already do, follow these tips to create a restful, meaningful spiritual retreat for your family.

o   Decide the Duration: Retreats can be anywhere from a half day to a week. Give yourself plenty of time to settle into the quiet and rest. Make sure there's plenty of time for rest, recreation and reflection.

o   Decide the Location: Pick a location that is far enough away to give you a feeling of being away. It could be to the lake north of town, a weekend in Chicago or a road trip to the mountains.

o   Loosely Plan the Activity: Don't cram the retreat full so that it feels like you're rushing from one thing to the next. Build in quiet moments of rest like lying down and looking for shapes in clouds, shooting stars at night or full-on naps in the hammocks. But also take advantage of the time to play together, whether that's yard games, water skiing, hiking or reading on a blanket under the shade tree.

o   Plan Time for Spiritual Formation as Individuals: Make sure everyone has something to do for their own quiet time(s). (For young children they might bring a picture bible.) Give ample time for each person to spend time alone with God reading the bible and praying, perhaps even journaling or reading a spiritual growth book as well. For little children, bring their picture Bible and books that they can read/look at quietly.

o   Plan Time for Family Spiritual Formation: This might be as simple as debriefing around the campfire what each person is learning in their own time, or it might be a study that you go through as a family.

o   Remember the Goal: Don't overcomplicate this so that you'll be more apt to repeat it. It's about rest, quiet time AWAY FROM activities, homework, chores and work, as well as quiet time WITH God and each other.

- **Make Family Outings Spiritual** - with a few simple tweaks, you can turn any restful/playful family outing into a meaningful spiritual formation activity. For example, read the creation story from Genesis 1 as you drive to the zoo. Discuss how your family will be involved in missions as you go fishing (fishers of men). On the way to the orchard, read Galatians 5:22 and discuss how the Holy Spirit bears fruit in our lives. With just a little thought, recreational outings you already take as a family can become meaningful times of influence.

CPSIA information can be obtained
at www.ICGtesting.com
Printed in the USA
LVHW04s1154160618
580379LV00001BD/1/P